ON THE NATURE OF LEADERSHIP

D1328592

Richard A. Barker

University Press of America,® Inc.
Lanham · New York · Oxford

To

Barbara

Table of Contents

Foreword

Written by
Joseph C. Rost

Richard Barker has written an important book on the nature of leadership. In my own writing on leadership, I stated that there is no more important work for leadership scholars and practitioners to accomplish than to determine what leadership is. Once we have determined the nature of leadership, we can then research, examine, develop, and practice it. Barker has taken up that challenge and has produced an extended statement developing his position on the fundamental nature of leadership. His scholarly analysis is a welcomed addition to the serious study of leadership, qua leadership, and those of us interested in developing a plausible theory of leadership will benefit greatly from his work.

The strengths of this book are many and varied. In the early part of the book, Barker's critical analysis of applying scientific canons to research "leadership" and the specific problems of using social science research assumptions to understand "leadership" make for interesting reading and reflection. In the end, Barker concludes that social science research "has failed to produce any meaningful understanding of leadership or any workable solutions to the problems the scholars who take this approach presume to address." While this conclusion has been stated before, Barker's penetrating analysis adds weight to this deconstructive view of the large body of leadership research conducted in the last century. If there can be no reconstruction until some deconstruction has occurred, there is plenty of meat in Barker's stew to stir the pot of misdirected and dysfunctional leadership research. The heat generated ought to help future leadership researchers pay very close attention to the nature of leadership before they research it.

The second strength is the discussion of conventional knowledge and how conventions influence our understanding and practice of leadership. The impact of conventions reappears throughout the book, and the reader cannot help but come away with a new, or at least a renewed, sense of the importance of conventions in the total scheme of things. Indeed, there is enough convention busting in this book to shake up conventional knowledge in various disciplines for some time!

A third strength is Barker's discussion of ethics and morals that pervade the book. Distinguishing between ethics and morals, Barker constantly hammers home the idea that the conjunction between one's ethics and the mores of the community is the space where leadership operates and transforms organizations. There are new concepts and practices to explore regarding the ethics of leadership in this book. Leadership scholars and practitioners need to look in a different direction, that is, away from traditional models and practices of leadership ethics, to solve the horrific problems facing postmodern organizations in this area.

A fourth strength is the indomitable courage Barker displays in his critique of the trappings of industrial leadership that inhabit thousands of research studies and how-to-do-it books sitting on the shelves of libraries and bookstores: traits, behaviors, styles, visions, goals, organizational culture, leaders causing effects, group dynamics, authority, prediction, power, success, effectiveness, greatness, contingencies and situations, management and supervision vs. leadership, and leader abilities. Again, this attack on the traditional view of leadership is constant and never-ending, from the first page to the last.

The fifth strength--and the book's greatest asset--is the explication of a new understanding of the nature of leadership, one that has substance, identity, coherence, and integrity. In Chapter 5, Barker develops a process definition of leadership and in Chapter 6 he articulates a relationship definition of leadership. Both are explained extensively and they are connected to one another. While carefully crafted, the definitions are complex and intricately woven into a realistic conceptual framework of leadership, one that simulates the messy, indeterminate, complicated, and difficult world of the 21st century.

Leadership books roll off the presses faster than any one person can possibly read them and remain current. Quantity, however, does not mean quality, and that is a significant problem. Publishers want leadership books to be quick and easy reads; books that one can pick up in the airport bookstore and finish by the time the plane arrives at its destination. I constantly sit on the floor in the management section of Barnes and Noble or Borders bookstores looking for something of substance and significance in the books purportedly about leadership. I spend hours on the Internet looking for leadership books that will possibly earn my respect and make me want to spend my hard-earned dollars to buy them. I am rarely satisfied with what I see and read. The books are mostly worthless and unproductive, they are inconsequential and simplistic, and most of them are not even about anything remotely resembling leadership.

On the Nature of Leadership is different. It's substantive and difficult reading; it is articulate and profound; it is critical and constructive; and it is really about leadership. Amazing! It is a work that will have a lasting impact on leadership studies, and I recommend it highly. Richard Barker has my respect and admiration.

Preface

This work will not find its place among that genre of books in which the typical book on leadership may be found. It will not provide the ambitious or the bewildered manager with tips on how to manage. There are no ready answers to questions of strategy and productivity. It will not provide the uninspired with easy steps to self-esteem. There are no quick solutions to life's complexities in these pages, nor are there trite formulas for increasing wealth, power, or control. While it is a work that is aimed at developing an understanding of leadership, more generally it represents my contribution, however minor, to "the long debate." At its core, it is an integrative exploration of complex social processes, and a sincere search for some explanation of subjects that seem to have defied previous attempts at articulating an understanding.

This book is not light reading; it does demand a degree of engagement and reflective consideration from the reader. It is not divided neatly into disciplinary compartments with bite-sized tidbits that are easily consumed and digested. However, it should be accessible to anyone with a broad, liberal education, and nothing developed here is beyond the grasp of the average person. Presumptions are made throughout that the reader is familiar with the foundational questions, debates, and issues prevalent in Western narrative traditions.

Criticism has been leveled at leadership studies for some decades for its failure to engage the important questions debated for the past three millennia., and for ignoring critical analysis. This work represents a critical analysis of the study of leadership, and I invite all debate upon its tenets.

This book is intended for those who really wish to know what leadership is. It is not intended for the traditional I-need-this-to-graduate course; it is not necessarily intended for those whose ambition is to become great corporate or civic leaders. It is intended for those who recognize the tendency for Western scholarship to oversimplify the conceptualization of social processes such as the one we call *leadership*, and for those who recognize that developing an understanding of these processes can lead to more effective problem solving.

Richard A. Barker
Fayette, Iowa
June, 2002

Acknowledgments

It would be impossible to acknowledge all of the sources used in the development of this treatise. Suffice it to say that very few, if any, of the ideas presented here are my ideas. The references cited are intended to acknowledge specific sources of ideas and to indicate where more fully developed arguments may be found.

The greatest debt is owed to Robert Pirsig, whom I have never met, who twice in my life provided the key to a door through which I needed to pass. Pirsig and Alan Watts are together the co-fathers of my approach to intellectual problems. Joseph Rost, whom I have met, is the father of that portion of my intellect which is devoted to the study of leadership, and William Foster is its favorite uncle. My thinking is most consistent with that of Bill Foster. But, the dialectic between Joe Rost and myself has been the most enlightening, lending support to Burns's notion that conflict is a critical element of leadership.

I must at this point acknowledge the contribution of Howard Manning, my fishing, motorcycle, and music partner and best friend for more than thirty years. It was Howard who finally convinced me to read *Zen and the Art of Motorcycle Maintenance* in the first place. That event brought about the means by which I was finally, at age 30, able to find success in my search for my identity. It was the true beginning of my scholastic career. Howard influenced my thinking and actions in very many ways. His talent, self-discipline, perseverance, and intellectual bent have always set the standards that I have endeavored to reach.

That said, I would not be whatever caliber of scholar I am today if not for Ray Loveridge, former Editor of *Human Relations*. His tolerance, encouragement, and helpful suggestions provided for the transformation of poorly organized ramblings into comprehensible argument. Professor Loveridge invited me to step up to a higher level of scholarship, and I accepted the invitation. Two of the three articles upon which this work is primarily based were direct outcomes of his tutelage. Whatever portion of this work that can be identified as good scholarship represents his legacy.

I must acknowledge the role of my wife, Barbara, without whose love and support none of this would have been possible (and I am not just saying that to get brownie points). I would like to acknowledge the rather difficult sacrifices my children, Jaime and Cory, made as a result of my pursuit of the course that has led to this outcome. I sincerely hope it was worth it. I would also like to thank my stepdaughter, Christina, for lending me her mother at a time when it was difficult for her to do that.

Finally, I must acknowledge the role my students for the past twenty five years have played as the sounding board for the development of most of these ideas. Though I have dragged them kicking and screaming through highly unstructured and difficult discussions and assignments, though I maintain a class motto of "suffering is good," they did not actually kill me. I am every student's worst nightmare--a reformed underachiever.

Introduction

Early in 1975, I was casting about for a thesis topic to finish up my MS in Industrial/Organizational Psychology. Upon the advice of others, I was searching for something quick and dirty with fancy statistics. In an age before computers, I had a knack for fancy statistics. I struck upon the newly arrived Path-Goal Theory of Leadership proposed by Robert House, and decided to conduct my study on leaders of music groups, to which I had access. Subordinate satisfaction was measured under conditions of leader directiveness and task ambiguity. A host of significant correlations supplemented by a significant three-way interaction barely filled twenty nine double spaced pages of text. The entire thesis was sixty pages including references, tables, graphs, appendices, and title pages, written in one weekend between Friday evening and Sunday afternoon. The binding was barely large enough to hold the complete title.

After the thesis was successfully defended with only a few minor changes, my advisor urged me to submit it for publication. I gave his suggestion some consideration, but finally realized that, having done this study, I knew nothing about leadership. The thesis was short because I had nothing to say about the subject. After all this work, I had learned nothing worth passing along. Fortunately, it did not bother me. It was a hokey topic that provided the vehicle for completion of my degree, and it led me on a path to the goal of getting a job.

My early career following graduation can best be described as checkered. It has not improved much even to the present day. The main reason for that is probably because I was never truly an employee, certainly never what anyone would refer to as a subordinate without experiencing some discomfort using that label. I have always given discomfort to those who presume to confer recognition for achievement.

I was, instead, a natural born social scientist who was living in the lab, an ethnographer studying strange people with strange customs, a proverbial Alice in a land of constant wonderment. Some of my bosses were able to take advantage of that; others were not. Over a span of fifteen years, I worked in manufacturing, in city government, in federal government, in computer services, and in aerospace. I held the titles of Research Data Analyst, Test Validation Analyst, Personnel Representative, Employment Manager, Industrial Engineer, Systems Analyst, Planning and Control Analyst, Material Specialist, Project Manager, Government Property Administrator, and Chair of the Picnic Committee (don't laugh, I had a $26,000 budget for the 1986 picnic). I was on the Safety Council, the Training Council, the Contract Closeout Red Team, and the Facilities Planning Committee. I was an Ethics Coordinator, a Standard Practices Coordinator, an EEO Coordinator, a Contingency Planner, a Quality Circle Facilitator, and a TQM Trainer. Besides the language of management, I learned to speak the language of systems development, the language of production control, the language of labor relations, the language of manufacturing, the language of proposal development, the language of material, and the language of government contracting. I was fluent in DAR, and FAR, and HRM, and SOCS, and IMS, and TDPS, and MPL, and MRPII, and SPC, and LVP, and SLCM, and ATS, and MILQ 9858A. During that time, I learned to observe, to analyze, and to explain without using statistics.

Before beginning doctoral studies under Joseph Rost, I asked him specifically if the leadership theories explored in his program were limited to those common to I/O psychology. He answered specifically that the goal of the program was to study leadership by every available method and viewpoint, and that the positivistic approach was less emphasized than other approaches. I enrolled immediately. I had the extreme fortune to begin the program alongside several gifted students who were equally anxious to make some meaning of leadership. The exchanges of ideas over the next three years was invigorating, and I emerged from that period of study with seeds of the directions taken in the following pages. That was twelve years ago.

What it takes to develop theory cannot be fully appreciated until one undertakes such an endeavor in earnest. Looking back, I am not convinced that it is a complete success. But, it is a step. It is a long step from that first mockery of science that I passed off as a masters thesis. At some point, you must shoot the engineers and get on with production.

The reader will encounter sections where the tone seems a bit pithy. That tone represents the frustration I feel toward those who have yet to realize what I have learned about leadership study--that it is not successfully accomplished through narrow measurements and fancy design. The reader may rest assured that at least some of the criticism has been justly earned by the targets of those comments.

No matter what your orientation, and given a sincere engagement with the following pages, you will never see leadership in the same way again.

Chapter 1

An Assessment of the Problem

"If we know all too much about our leaders, we know far too little about *leadership*" (Burns, 1978, p. 1). Thus, Burns introduced us to his rationale for exploring a new perspective--a revolutionary new paradigm he called transforming leadership. Burns was clearly trying to imply that *leadership* is something different from *leaders*, that is leader traits and behaviors. This intent is evident in his final definition of leadership: "leadership is the reciprocal process of mobilizing, by persons with certain motives and values, various economic, political, and other resources, in a context of competition and conflict, in order to realize goals independently or mutually held by both leaders and followers" (p. 425).

The two keys to this definition that seem to have escaped many current writers who discuss transformational leadership are first his admonition that the nature of the goals is crucial--that is if they are not mutual they may be independently held, but in any case they must be related and oriented toward an end value--and second the process is reciprocal and it happens within a context of competition and conflict. Burns, a political scientist, introduced perspectives used in the political sciences to understand and to explain individual, organizational, and societal outcomes of social processes.

But what have we done with the study of leadership in the years since Burns made these propositions and encouraged us to use different perspectives? We have reduced it to slogans: "Managers are people who do things right and leaders are people who do the right thing" (Bennis & Nanus, 1985, p. 21). We have equated it with economic success and with manipulating people: "Leadership is measured by success and effectiveness. A leader is successful when the person he or she is trying to influence demonstrates the desired behavior" (Forbes, 1991, p. 70). We have confused it with management and with supervision: "Successful leaders and managers must use power--to influence others, to monitor results, and to sanction performance" (Winter, 1991, p. 77). We have associated it with authority: "Leadership has traditionally been synonymous with authority, and authority has traditionally been understood as the ability to command others, control subordinates, and make all the truly important decisions yourself" (Katzenbach & Smith, 1992, p. 129). We have become mired in an obsession with the rich and powerful, with traits, characteristics, behaviors, roles, styles, and abilities of people who by hook or by crook have obtained high positions, and we know little if anything more about *leadership*: "Students of leadership will be interested in shedding light on the dominant background characteristics of the elite, their homogeneity, and behavioral patterns" (Bassiry & Dekmejian, 1993, p. 47).

Western politicians advocate self-reliance as the answer to problems of social and economic welfare. The media are full of themes that glorify self-directed rule breakers--the rogue cop, the unscrupulous but successful entrepreneur, and the bold outlaw--all of which celebrate the independence of will and of action that characterize "the one who stands alone." There are virtually no themes of teamwork in politics, in the media, or in education. Even when teams are portrayed, their success or failure is commonly attributed to one individual's actions. In professional sports, players are regarded for their personal statistics and not for team performance.

Virtually every definition of leadership one finds in both scholarly and practitioner-oriented writings--that is if a definition is actually offered--focuses on the knowledge, skills, abilities, and traits of the leader which are presumed to most successfully result in followers doing what the leader wants them to do (Rost, 1991). Consider this quote by DuBrin (1990): "Leaders influence people to do things through the use of power and authority" (p. 257). Even though DuBrin defined leadership as "the process of influencing the activities of an individual or group to achieve certain objectives in a given situation" (p. 255), it is clear that he was conceptualizing the *process* of leadership as a linear set of goal-oriented actions by the leader, and certainly not in the same plane as the process of conflict and competition described by Burns (1978). At least DuBrin offered a definition. Not defining leadership seems to be an accepted practice among scholars who discuss leadership. Rost (1991) analyzed a total of 587 works that referred to leadership in their titles and found that fully 366 of them did not specify any definition of leadership. Those authors apparently assumed that everyone knows what leadership is.

Where we have gone wrong.

Leadership studies in the past few decades have been the subject of increasing criticism for maintaining outmoded constructs and for bearing less than scholastic integrity (Burns, 1978; Foster, 1986; Gemmill & Oakley, 1992; Rost, 1991). At a leadership conference some years ago, faculty members of internationally known leadership education programs involved themselves in a discussion about what to call leadership: is it an art, a study, a discipline, a theoretical construct, what? The discussion was interrupted by the dinner speaker who inadvertently answered the question by declaring that leadership is an industry. This answer may indicate something about the mounting criticism, that is, that the selling of leadership training and education has created an a priori agenda for research and conclusions about leadership. However, the problems of leadership study are not quite as simple as that.

The problems of leadership study are complicated by paradigms of economics and social organization the origins of which extend thousands of years into the past. Simply put, these paradigms establish the economic and social roles of the leader, but do nothing to explain the nature of the phenomenon we call *leadership*. As a result, the term *good leadership* can refer to dramatically different forms of social outcomes. For example,

(1) leadership can refer to a situation where social status and wealth have been enhanced, such as winning a football game or increasing stock value;

(2) leadership can refer to a situation where one has been inspired to work toward a greater intangible good, such as volunteering in a hospital or marching to protest in support of civil rights; or,

(3) leadership can refer to a situation where something superior in quality has been experienced, such as leadership in seafood.

Old ideas about the structure and purpose of social hierarchies establish the superiority of the leader, and are tenaciously held by those who have worked hard to attain leadership positions and their associated status. Scholars who aspire to increase their own social and economic standing are irresistibly drawn into the prostitution of their craft--a temptation that all who aspire to greatness must abide. Modern leadership scholars seem to be enraptured by old and unquestioned ways of thinking because they must pander to the will and whim of the *leaders* who would buy their services. The result is a self-reinforcing cycle of internally constructed reality that stubbornly refuses to change with the times.

Just as most English-speaking people use the word *classical* to refer to any music associated with symphonic or chamber ensembles, most people use the word *leadership* to refer to any activities or relationships associated with persons occupying top positions in a hierarchy. Yet the words Classical, referring to music of the Classical Period, and leadership are indicative each of a specific phenomenon. Music scholars ignore popular terminology and carefully specify and define music according to its style, its form, its content, and its function, conceptually separating the structure, style, and experience of what is Classical from what is Baroque and from what is Romantic. Most leadership scholars have no such clearly defined formal taxonomy, and make no serious attempt to distinguish what they are studying from popular misconceptions (Rost, 1991).

There are those who would argue that distinguishing charismatic leadership from, say, servant leadership has accomplished the goal of classification. But, to use the music analogy, it is the same as distinguishing one of Mozart's symphonies from one of Haydn's symphonies. They are both examples of the same Classical form with differences which do not distinguish the form from other forms. Classical is one of many forms of music organization, which can be distinguished from other sound phenomena. Leadership is one of many forms of social organization, which can be distinguished from other human behavior phenomena.

The need to distinguish leadership from other forms of social organization, such as management or politics, is roughly the same as the need to distinguish Classical music from other forms of music organization, such as Baroque or Romantic. It matters to the extent that people act upon their understandings. A correct classification of music or of leadership means little to the person who is merely enjoying the experience. But it means a great deal to someone who is teaching others who will then be the participants in the creation of music or of leadership. Therefore, the distinction must be made using analysis that is consistent with its experiential nature, yet sufficient to make the distinction. In short, it must be phenomenological and metaphysical, and not merely quantitative.

Theories of leadership that place the leader at the center of the leadership process are similar to geocentric theories that place the earth at the center of the universe. It does not matter to the casual observer who sees the sun moving across the sky whether or not it revolves around the earth. It does matter if the observer is interested in space exploration or in making certain predictions based upon the position of the sun. Activities conducted from a particular understanding necessarily change if that understanding changes. Theory matters only to those who must use that theory to take action, then the truth of the theory must be measured by its application. Application of leader-centered theory has made little contribution other than to enrich consultants, authors, and trainers and to inflate those who consider themselves leaders. The leader is but one of many planets revolving around the sum of human wills.

At the end of his massive compilation of the *experimenta lucifera* that passes for leadership research, Bass (1990) asserted that those who bemoan the inconclusiveness of the evidence and the subsequent dearth of understanding of leadership should be quieted by the shear volume of pages of leadership findings. Yet, nowhere in his book did Bass make a serious attempt to articulate an ontological foundation for leadership study. His position, as is usually the case with industrial leadership scholars, was that application of method necessarily confers ontological standing. While he acknowledged the existence of other views, Bass, like so many others, relied upon the dominant paradigm to be self-evident, and to be the view of choice for the future. This unquestioning reliance is likely the result of a vested interest in the old thinking. Could it be that leadership scholars are not really scholars, but marketing representatives, developing programs for consumption by persons with business and political ambitions? Or, are leadership scholars simply less sophisticated than their counterparts in the physical sciences in developing *experimenta frutifera*, so that competing theories may be examined?

It is possible that the mainstream concept of leadership provides a "social defense whose central aim is to repress uncomfortable needs, emotions, and wishes that emerge when people attempt to work together" (Gemmill & Oakley, 1992, p. 114). Gemmill and Oakley made an excellent case for the notion that leadership is an ideology designed to support the existing social order by providing both a rationale for dysfunction and a direction in which to shift blame. Given that this is the case, then there would be no need for scholars to define leadership specifically. Indeed, there is incentive to avoid any precision that would explode the myth that certain individuals in a social system are entitled to a greater share of the wealth and power by virtue of their *leadership abilities*, which are more often established by association than by deed.

Not surprising is the nearly universal silence among leadership scholars on these compelling arguments and conclusions presented over a decade ago. There has been virtually no debate on these issues primarily because they erode the foundations of the leadership industry, and because they are difficult to refute other than to say "I disagree." It is tempting to cease all serious investigation in light of Gemmill and Oakley's conclusions, surrendering leadership study to the sphere of science occupied by pop management, evangelism, and astrology. Yet within complex social processes of change, movements, or revolutions, there seems to be something foundational that generates the experience often called *leadership*. How are we to understand those phenomena that bring us together and inspire us to transcend our ordinary existence and do greater things? What word do we apply to that which people felt during the American and French Revolutions, during the Civil Rights Movement, in China under Mao, during the American Civil War, or in France, in America, in England, even in Germany during World War II, and in countless other times, circumstances, and places? An explanation could be devised as long as it shifts its focus away from the exclusive few toward the inclusive many.

It is difficult to imagine a Zen master contemplating leadership. To those who are truly enlightened, the issues of ontology and epistemology regarding social phenomena must be of little consequence. For the rest of us, there is hope that something of meaning and value can be discovered beyond the celebration, in the mindless drivelworks that often pass for management literature, of executives, politicians, and football coaches who are shamelessly paraded before us as archetypes of great leadership.

There is new thinking in the physical sciences and in philosophy that is challenging the historic, philosophical foundations of scientific theories. Old theories of leadership, management, and administration are contained within the Newtonian language and logical positivism of the old physical sciences that are not consistent with new ideas about the nature of reality and of life. As a result, there is a loosely coupled set of ideas and findings that indicate some fundamental transitions in our thinking about a new administrative science (Overman, 1996). These new sciences demand an examination of old assumptions and the application of new perspectives to that which we understand as leadership.

It will be the contention of this discussion that most authors are unaware of their reliance upon a very old paradigm of leadership as well as upon other old paradigms. These old paradigms conflict with the realities of the modern world in a way that decreases effective problem solving. This discussion is not as much a critique of specifically articulated theories of leadership as it is a criticism of the constructual framework that has been used to develop those theories. The essential construct of leadership will be examined both in its current failure to solve the problems most leadership scholars address, and in its promise as a theory of explanation that has implications for practitioners.

The Scientific Approach to Understanding Leadership

For most of the 20th Century, the applications of sciences founded in the reconstruction of philosophy during the Age of Enlightenment have been systematically deconstructed and examined. While this discussion has little to add to the argument that Cartesian science is inadequate for application to the social sciences, it would be instructive to develop a contextual framework for that argument to be used for the examination of leadership study in particular and of social sciences methodology in general. Such a development, for or against, has, for the most part, been neglected by those who claim to study leadership.

Scientific study is accomplished by the creation of a metaphysical canon of consistency used primarily for structuring research and for developing educational curricula to perpetuate the study (Harré, 1970; Kuhn, 1970). The canon of industrial-era leadership theories is an adaptation of the hierarchical view of the universe adopted by the early Christian Church, and presumes that leadership concerns first, the person at the top of a hierarchy, who has been "anointed by God," second, this person's exceptional (usually male-like, certainly god-like) qualities and abilities to manage the structure and outcomes of this hierarchy, and third, the activities of this person in relation to goal achievement. This canon is then incorporated into pragmatic application of theory. For example, the industrial theories of leadership based in an assumption of specialized leadership abilities are used to justify high executive salaries.

The canon of any discipline is the conceptual basis for the professional language, and is founded in specific metaphysical assumptions which are defended and perpetuated as the *truth* (Harré, 1970). Another name for this truth is *conventional knowledge*. As with any model of science, the language used to discuss leadership consists of specific descriptive terms that are designed to regulate the discipline by copying or representing a particular paradigm. Terms such as transformational, transactional, servant, charismatic, and strategic are attached to the word *leadership* to represent the industrial paradigm. Each of these descriptive terms perpetuates the dominant construct by indicating some variation of the industrial model of leadership.

The industrial model describes the characteristics and activities of a high status person (a) who is different from the rest of us, (b) who sits atop a hierarchy, (c) who can control outcomes and help us *win*, (d) who gives us hope for salvation, (e) who has a *vision* (read goals) that we should pursue, (f) who employs some set of behaviors and influencing motifs to entice us to pursue that vision, and (g) who will take some action toward the resolution of specific organizational or social problems. Each of the descriptive terms mentioned above refer, to one degree or another, to each of these elements.

The influence of the industrial paradigm of leadership is so compelling that many authors feel no need to define the term *leadership*. The industrial view has become a permanent fact upon which leadership theories are supposed to be built. The differing categorical terms of leadership all use the same model as a source for their meaning and application. In other words, the function of each of the terms commonly used in industrial language is to indicate a variation of the form "man at the top," and how that form is manifested. The term *leadership* is defined ostensively while pointing to someone who occupies a high position, and the epistemology of leadership is limited to comparisons of the characteristics of one leader with another. Leadership study, then, has become simple Baconian fact-finding designed to reinforce the industrial paradigm, and to nullify competing theories.

Scientists develop firm answers to basic metaphysical questions before they begin research (Kuhn, 1970). The answers to these questions indicate the scientist's assumptions about the nature of the universe, about how its entities interconnect, about what can legitimately be asked about these entities and their interrelationships, about what counts as knowledge, about how knowledge is discovered, and so forth. Through these beliefs, the scientist structures and articulates the problems to be solved, specifies the data to be analyzed, creates the methodology used to gather and to analyze data, and proposes directions that the conclusions should take. In the social sciences, beliefs about human nature, about a person's meaning in the context of the universe, about the human condition, about what is wrong with people, and about how social and personal problems can be remedied lead scientists to develop some model of psychology and some theory of social context from which behavior can be interpreted.

Social sciences have developed with many of the fundamental assumptions about reality used in the physical sciences (Harré, Clarke, & DeCarlo, 1985). Science has two basic functions: to explain what has happened, and to predict what will happen. The ultimate goal of science is to predict, given that accurate prediction makes life easier. To facilitate prediction, Cartesian science assumes the existence of mechanistic, deterministic, cause-effect relationships that can be replicated in equivalent circumstances because they follow immutable laws. These relationships depend for their analysis upon distinctions between subjects and objects. It makes no sense to discuss one thing causing another unless the two *things* can be distinguished. Two *things* are distinguished by the nature of their substance; they have distinctive properties. Before modern quantum physics, substance was simply thought to be matter. But measurements of quanta have drawn into question that even material objects have any identifiable or consistent "substance" (Capra, 1983).

In social sciences, the *substance* used to distinguish subject from object has been a sometimes confusing mixture of two categories of substance: (a) properties of biological units or sets of biological units and (b) properties of their behavior. The science of behavior has portrayed itself as empirical because properties of substance (units and their behavior) are observed and measured. However, behavior cannot be sliced up, pasted on a slide, and placed under the microscope for observation of its properties. Behavior is measured by applying assumptions about the purpose of the behavior, and by interpreting intentions and meaning. Observation of behavior is conducted by sorting out its increments. Dividing behavior into discrete units for study creates the same metaphysical problems as that approach does for any continuous phenomenon, such as for motion or for history.

Prediction is not always possible with scientific theory, even if cause-effect relationships can be established. For example, the theory of evolution can explain what has happened, but cannot predict what new species will inevitably result from combinations of genetic mutation and environmental conditions. The problem of studying complex and continuous social processes falls into this realm of explanation without prediction. The ontological nature of the problem was delineated nicely by Leo Tolstoy (1952) in the first chapter of Book Eleven of *War and Peace*. His observation was that the science of history is plagued by certain metaphysical issues. Specifically, he began with an illustration of the absurdity of breaking down motion into discontinuous parts for study, and the resulting conclusion of certain ancient Greeks that Achilles could never catch a tortoise even though he was ten times as fast because the tortoise would always be ahead of him by an increment of one tenth. The conclusion is absurd because there is inevitable error made by the human mind when it contemplates separated elements rather than the continuous whole. The error is made with the assumption that each increment has a beginning and an end; Achilles cannot reach the tortoise because each is thought to be reaching an end point at the same time, which necessarily separates them by a discrete increment.

Leadership studies are commonly subject to the same erroneous assumptions as studies of history. History, like motion, is examined by isolating events or series of events into increments as though they have absolute beginnings and ends, and as though they are subject to cause-effect relationships. The first error of history, according to Tolstoy, is the assumption that a collection of these discrete events is the equivalent of continuous history. The second error of history is the assumption that the actions of one person (king, conqueror, etc.) is the equivalent of many individual wills.

> Historians . . . lay before us the sayings and doings of a few dozen men in a building in the city of Paris, calling these sayings and doings "the Revolution;" then they give a detailed biography of Napoleon and of certain people favorable or hostile to him; tell of the influence some of these people had on others, and say: that is why this movement took place. But . . . this method of explanation is fallacious, because in it a weaker phenomenon is taken as the cause of a stronger. The sum of human wills produced the Revolution and Napoleon, and only the sum of those wills first tolerated and then destroyed them. (p. 470)

As with history and motion, the integrity of the *substance* of social science is tenuous, and the intangible character of the substance plays havoc with method. Sometimes what is measured in one unit is thought to represent measurements expected in all similar units [1. properties among units are assumed to be the same]. Sometimes units are differentiated by what is measured [2. properties among units are assumed to be different]. Sometimes a single unit is differentiated from itself by comparing its measurements at Time 1 with those at Time 2 [3. properties measured in a single unit can be expected to vary over time]. Social and intellectual patterns outside of those indicated by a unit's behavior do not have measurable properties and so are not thought to have substance. Therefore, any exploration of values or feelings or collective influences is considered subjective (without substance) and not objective.

The basic philosophical question of substance is whether matter is created by the mind (idealism) or the mind is created by matter (materialism) (Russell, 1972). Positivism, the philosophical position of empirical science, does not consider the issue important enough to argue (Pirsig, 1991): matter is what we measure empirically and not what we judge or abstract from experience. Matter is necessarily assumed not to contain value. Value, if it exists, is thought to be attached to matter after it is observed and analyzed. Value is thought to be interpreted from the analysis of data according to an abstract, intellectual, and subjective judgement.

Yet, empiricism begins with a direct observation, which is to say that it begins with a human perception of a phenomenon. Even if an instrument is used, the existence of the substance of the phenomenon is verified by a perception of data supplied by the instrument. Observations do not exist independent from the observer (Locke, 1947). Contrary to positivist assertions, a direct observation is necessarily founded in a particular *value* that is experienced before the observation itself or any abstract intellectualization or analysis can begin. Some value, for example, is behind the attention to the observation in the first place. Why is the scientist studying this instead of that?

Value can be defined as a preferred outcome or state of existence, but there is much more to it than that. In his development of the Metaphysics of Quality, Pirsig (1991) revolutionized the concept of value by naming it a relationship, and imbuing this relationship with ontological standing in the manner of mathematical relationships. As opposed to a simple idea of preference, value can be considered a fundamental building block for all physical and metaphysical explanations of the universe. Value replaces matter as the essential substance that can be used to explain all material phenomena. Pirsig's idea is not entirely consistent with materialistic "corpuscular" theories; value is the stuff, but not material stuff--value may be consistent over time, but not necessarily. Value is understood beyond its role as a component of preferential relationships to be the source of those relationships.

Investigations of phenomena are generated by deep seated, persistent values that are experienced at both instinctual and cognitive levels before any assessment of empirical validity can take place. Pirsig used the example of a scientist sitting on a hot stove to illustrate the role of value in observation. Regardless of the scientist's philosophical persuasion, the scientist will jump off the hot stove and exclaim some oaths, thus declaring that the phenomenon has negative value. The values in question are not abstract intellectual or religious constructs, but fundamental attractions such as the value a positively charged ion has for a negatively charged ion.

The scientist's declaration of negative value is not a metaphysical abstraction, or a subjective judgement, or a description of a subjective experience; it is a predictable, verifiable, empirical observation. In other words, the *value* is present before the *observation* takes place. Positivism proclaims that the stove *causes* the behavior of the scientist which then indicates value. But according to Pirsig, the value lies between the stove and the exclamation. The scientist's behavior is more likely caused by the value than by the stove, but in any case the reality of causation is constructed after the phenomenon occurs. And, there is no hint of substance unless one is willing to consider *value* as substance. Empirical observations begin with perceptions of value.

Substance apart from its properties cannot be proven to exist; substance is what it is experienced to be (Locke, 1947). The existence of any substance is verified through the experience of patterns of data. Pirsig suggested that we strike the term *substance* and instead use the phrase *stable pattern of value*. Rather than using properties of substance to distinguish a *thing* like leadership from other things, one can use a pattern of value to make the same distinction. Distinguishing leadership from other things by using a pattern of value will necessarily establish the reality of the *thing* we call leadership.

The essential nature of leadership can then be determined through patterns of value, both stable and dynamic. Leadership may be thought to be a biological pattern (traits), or an intellectual pattern (knowledge and ability), but it might be more instructive to think of it as a social pattern of value. There are many different social patterns of applied value, and the patterns that may be identified as leadership will be discussed further.

The Specific Problems of Social Science Research

The industrial paradigm of leadership has been created and maintained as an application of science, the implicit goal of which has been to perpetuate important feudal institutions of power and authority in society. It is this goal of leadership study that has created its scientific inconsistencies, and has limited its adaptation to changing environments. Positivistic leadership theories are presumed to incorporate the Cartesian deductive system, and the development of those theories has been predicated on several assumptions common to science. Positivism as applied to models of human behavior in contemporary psychology suffers from several outmoded assumptions that restrict the ability of its adherents to accept changing paradigms of human behavior and of science in general (Harré, Clark, & DeCarlo, 1985).

First is the assumption that the truth of human behavior may be discovered through scientism. Contemporary psychology relies almost exclusively on research methodologies derived from the physical sciences, all of which are based in the Cartesian deductive system. The limitations of this system are recognized even in the physical sciences (Capra, 1983; Harré, 1970). The essential limitation of the Cartesian system is its assumption that all phenomena are governed by physical laws, which may be derived using empirical methods.

Descartes' method of critical doubt implies two things (Russell, 1972): First, knowledge derived by logic must ultimately end with indisputable principles of inference. Second, knowledge derived from empirical methods must end with indisputable facts. Both of these points imply that thought is the primary realm of certainty, and that there is ultimately no end to science because nothing will ever be indisputable. The supposition is that there are two worlds--that of the mind, and that of matter--which can be studied independently, without reference to each other. Another important supposition is that the world, even its living organisms, is essentially deterministic, and governed by the laws of physics.

Those who maintain that all phenomena are governed by physical laws do not perceive any limitations to what is broadly called scientific method. Investigations into social phenomena that restrict themselves to scientific methods rarely result in anything more than shedding light on narrow aspects, given that light is shed from a viewpoint which leaves some portion of the subject in the dark. This approach does not allow for comprehensive understanding of a phenomenon simply because it cannot access its entirety. Disassembling a mountain for study does not allow for an understanding of the interrelationships among creatures living on the mountain, or between the mountain and the weather. To those who accept that some properties of phenomena are not accessible through scientific method, there is potential for a grasp of improbable and unmeasurable influences to affect measurement outcomes. In other words, stuff happens that is not logical or measurable, and behavior is influenced by nonphysical phenomena. Inferential methods used by research psychologists can only be partially useful.

Leadership is usually treated as a Platonic form--that is, it has been granted ontological standing by virtue of its attribution to those individuals who reside at the top of a hierarchy. Study of leadership has been conducted by reducing the whole to its basic elements for study. These elements have been assumed to be traits and characteristics of the leader and situational variables. Methods used to determine traits are validated by the traits they dredge up, and having arrived at measured traits investigators are encouraged to attribute validity to the idea that traits are the substance of leadership. The idea determines the method, and the method in turn validates the idea.

The assumption that the whole is represented by its elements may be appropriate for some studies: for example, a molecular study of granite. But reducing a music composition into its notes and measures cannot possibly lead to an adequate understanding or theory about the experience of hearing it. It may be equally unreasonable to assume that social phenomena like leadership can be understood by isolating foundational components. Leadership, like music, has experiential qualities and continuity that defy deductive analysis.

The second outmoded assumption commonly held in contemporary psychology, according to Harré, et al., is that each individual person is a unit within which all important psychological processes occur, and that psychological measurements of an individual are valid as stand-alone measurements. Under this assumption, the behavior of each individual unit (person), even if it is measured under isolated lab conditions, is thought to be representative of long-term, consistent patterns that exist in social behavior. The superior/subordinate dyadic relationship of the transactional model of leadership is characteristic of this assumption. The model defines dyads as two separate and independently functioning units (people) that are capable of operating in relation to each other without outside social influences. This relationship is thought to exist everywhere as it is measured in one instance. The dyadic model defines groups as collections of individuals who are independent even when they interact face-to-face (Yammarino, 1995). There is virtually no mechanism to detect or to explain the interactive effects of complex social influences on behavior.

An assumption of constancy is applied to studies of the leader as a unit. For example, if a leader is honest at the time of measurement, then it has been assumed that the trait of honesty is present when successful leadership is occurring. But this assumption has two problems: first, individual traits are not necessarily consistent over time and through varying conditions, and second, one does not know when successful leadership is actually occurring. Rost (1991) addressed this problem by trying to define the circumstances of the occurrence of leadership.

The third outmoded assumption is that because individuals are self-contained, measurable units, what is measured in one individual is universally applicable to all individuals regardless of their social or cultural context. The limitation of this common psychological assumption as it applies to the transformational leadership model was addressed, although superficially, by Jung, Bass, and Sosik (1995). Jung, et al. examined the implications of the model for collectivistic cultures where superior and subordinate role expectations and the motivation to work and to behave may be governed by principles not indicated by psychological research conducted in North America.

The fourth outmoded assumption is related to the first; that is, physical effects must necessarily have causes. The desire to establish mechanisms for organizational manipulation and control have led transformational leadership enthusiasts to focus exclusively on linear cause-effect relationships. The emerging paradigm of leadership acknowledges that some observable outcomes are not necessarily the result of direct, linear, or simply defined causes. Rather, they are phenomena that emerge from processes so complex that they cannot be adequately represented by linear models (correlation coefficients) or by simple descriptive concepts such as dyadic relationships.

Leadership is normally studied with the specific goal of determining cause-effect relationships. This approach relies upon the belief that causality is found in a regularity of sequence. But there can be no evidence that given sequences of events are not merely accidental or arbitrary, particularly when they occur in complex milieus like organizations and societies. Linear models do not account for complex influences on social outcomes. Further, there is generally little consistency in the interpretations of such sequences. The industrial paradigm of leadership depends upon the existence of cause-effect relationships for its validity. The failure to establish firmly any casual relationships does support the view that they do not exist. The approach taken in this discussion pursues a broad comprehension of the whole, and rejects deduction as a useful method.

The search for cause-effect relationships is expected to yield some degree of predictability and control. Industrial leadership studies have developed under the same optimism as earthquake studies, that prediction and control of outcomes is ultimately possible even though critical parameters are highly complex and potentially unknowable. This discussion will deemphasize prediction as a central theme.

The problems of logical positivism in social science research can be summed up by the term *error variance*. Error variance is used to explain all those observations that do not fit the hypothesis. It is needed to smooth out epistemological inconsistencies. Conclusions may be supported according to accepted probabilities, but how can all this error be explained? A correlation between some measure of leader authenticity and some measure of morale can be significant at the $p<.01$ level even if it is only .44 (Henderson & Brookhart, 1996). But if leader authenticity actually causes morale, a much higher level of correlation would be expected. What would we understand about gravity if a dropped pencil fell to earth only half the time? This approach to explaining relationships does little to uncover the actual nature of the relationship. A relationship of .44 should indicate, if anything, that it has not been explained completely, and that something is more influential to morale than leader authenticity.

Ultimately, reductionism leads to asking the wrong questions--such as asking what station a radio is tuned in to when it is not plugged in, or asking what the radio is for and then attempting to answer the question by disassembling it. A well calculated and well supported answer to the wrong question does little to reveal truth. A century of faltering with the Cartesian approach has yet to persuade leadership scholars that they need to change the questions as well as the methods used for answering them. It may be that discovery of truth is not their main objective. Certainly, valid criticisms of leadership study have been roundly ignored by most authors of leadership books and articles, and in some cases actively suppressed by those who control access to journals, conferences, and discussion media. This conspiracy of denial does support the notion that the field is an industry that rejects any serious inquiry which might interfere with commerce.

In summary, the term *leadership* has been here-to-fore defined ostensively by pointing to a person occupying a high or authoritative position. This approach has failed to produce any meaningful understanding of leadership or any workable solutions to the problems the scholars who take this approach presume to address. Leadership in the emerging paradigm is ostensively defined by pointing to group processes. This paradigm will prove to be unapproachable using the Cartesian theory of explanation, which for many reductionists is reason enough to reject it altogether. Then again, reductionism has not provided anything useful beyond the enrichment of a few individuals regardless of its propensity for research. Leader characteristics and behaviors are readily measurable, and so have been embraced by industrial-era leadership studies. But there have been no consistent results that have led to anything like a solid theory of leadership based in characteristics of the leader.

A Different Analogy

The phenomenon of *leadership* must be distinguished from the activities, functions, and characteristics of the leader often labeled as leadership. As will be argued later, these activities, functions, and characteristics are more appropriately understood as supervision, command, management, and statesmanship. Bringing the distinction to the awareness of conventional thinkers is no mean task. The following analogy has been constructed to illustrate the distinction, and to suggest a structure for the discussion.

When a conventional thinker is asked to describe the manner in which a ship represents leadership, the answers I have encountered usually begin with the captain. The captain plans, organizes, directs, and controls the activities of the crew to bring about outcomes, specifically the ship's direction. In some such descriptions, influences other than the captain are acknowledged to have some role, but in general the captain is thought to be the specific cause of the ship's direction and the crew to be followers who carry out the captain's commands.

The leader, however, is best represented by the bow of the ship, and is not the primary determinant of outcomes. The bow is out in front, and usually points in the direction that the ship is traveling, but has relatively little to do with determining the ship's direction. The directional outcome of the ship is the result of interactions among many factors. First among these factors is that which drives the ship, the engine. The engine represents the sum of human wills, and it is fueled by value, the sort of which is described above. The engine drives the ship headlong in the direction it is pointed, and the preponderance of the outcome is the result of the engine doing, or not doing, its work.

Of some importance in determining the ship's direction is the vessel itself. The vessel contains the engine and all relevant internal systems, and represents the social structure of the group in question. The nature and design of the vessel have a great deal to do with the ship's response to management and to the application of power and control. The vessel offers some degree of responsiveness to external forces--the water, seaweed, the current, and the wind. The degree of responsiveness depends upon the relationship of the design to its context, and upon other factors such as the accumulation of barnacles, distortions in the hull, cracks, leaks, etc. The vessel can be light and fast, or slow and awkward. It can be easily maneuverable, or difficult to maneuver. It can be easily swamped or impossible to capsize. The vessel can be pointed in the direction it is going entirely by outside forces--the wind and the current.

The vessel is steered to varying degrees of success, given varying conditions, by the rudder. The rudder represents the sum total of management applied to the operations of the ship. In some small vessels, steering is accomplished by direct manipulation of the engine, and there is no rudder. In other small vessels, the rudder is directly connected to the till, and can be operated effectively by simple manipulations from a single individual. In large ships, the rudder is separated from the steering apparatus by some combination of servos, pulleys, ropes, motors, gears, and other devices. In very large ships, response time is so long and feedback so slow that steering requires a team of people with sophisticated tools to calculate the appropriate application of control. Too few resources applied to the steering of large ships can result in a direction determined by some combination of inside as well as outside forces. Disagreement over the application of controls and misjudgment are examples of inside forces. In some vessels, the manager can see immediate results of applied control, but many factors may potentially reduce effective control. The rudder mechanism may be well designed and efficient, or poorly designed and unreliable.

Finally, there is that which differentiates the concept of leadership from most other social systems and processes, the question of purpose. In what direction should the ship be traveling and, more importantly, why? The captain and crew do not usually make that determination. The captain may facilitate maneuvers around obstacles like sand bars and icebergs, but not decide what ports to enter or whether the ship is to fight battles, to engage in commerce, to explore the sea, or simply to transport something from one point to another. To make this analogy work, we must assign the determination of purpose to the fuel for the engine--value, or more precisely, shared value. Fuel has a number of sources and comes in a number of forms.

The ship analogy (a curse on anyone who calls it "the leader-ship") is intended to illustrate a difference between old thinking and new thinking. So often, when authors claim to have a new perspective on leadership, it is the same old perspective with some new words substituted for old words. The remainder of this discussion will attend to the elements of the ship analogy.

Chapter 2

The Engine of Leadership: Theories of Conduct

It is with great peril that one understands the engine of leadership as something mechanical. The engine of leadership can only be characterized as a process--black box, if you will--that converts energy into motion, and all references to mechanisms must be abandoned at least until mechanical elements of the process can be distinguished from nonmechanical elements.

Developing a construct of the engine must necessarily incorporate a discussion of the fuel for the engine--value and purpose. A complete understanding of leadership must include topics not usually addressed in books on the subject, such as the development of moral thought. Understanding what leadership is and how it works proceeds, in the same manner that Plato understood politics, from an understanding of people-- how they are constituted and how they pursue the ends of life. How ends are procured is the primary subject of moral theory, and understanding the development of moral thought lends insight to investigations of social processes. As with all such developments, errors will necessarily be made on the side of oversimplification and overgeneralization.

Where Shall We Begin?

"In the beginning was the Word" (John 1:1). Before there was wisdom; before there were lessons to teach and to learn; before there were rules to follow; there was the *point* of it all. To Christians, the *point* is God. The wisdom and the lessons and the rules are all used as means to serve God. That is the *point*. At something less than a cosmic level, there is a *point* to be considered with every human endeavor. This *point* may be agreeable to all, or it may be an issue of contention among both observers and participants. The *point* is not the same as ends, goals, and objectives. The points made in an argument are not the same as the *point* of arguing in the first place.

What is the *point* of studying leadership? To some, the point is to identify and train leaders, such that productivity may be increased. To others, the point is to find some way of increasing their personal status through an association with the word *leadership*. These are not *points*, but goals and objectives. The *point* of studying leadership is to come to grips with what it means to be a human in society with other humans--it is an experience the nature of which changes over time. The goal of studying leadership is assumed to be an increased understanding of the human condition, such that our social problems may be more meaningfully addressed, and perhaps more readily solved. The *point* of studying leadership is akin to the *point* of studying ethics. "We are inquiring not in order to know what virtue is, but in order to become good, since otherwise our inquiry would have been of no use" (Aristotle, 1961, II,2).

Conventional Knowledge

Critical philosophy is itself an artifact of Western culture. No other civilization has traditions recognized as philosophical by Western philosophers. Other cultures consider the same questions, but use dramatically different approaches in answering them. There are many reasons for these cultural differences, but a complete treatment of the subject is beyond the scope of this discussion, and not critical to the understanding of leadership.

Modern Western moral theories are founded in normative traditions of rational development (Rasmussen, 1993). Rasmussen, in a critique of post-modernism, concluded that if modern moral theories are not targeted for rehabilitation, then the result is not an ethic. However, normative traditions are valid only within a specific cultural context, and their rehabilitation is an adaptation of moral theory to cultural change and a continuation of conventional reasoning.

A case for extending any moral theory beyond cultural boundaries must be made as part of the theory. To make that extension, common human experiences and the context of those experiences must be taken into account (Finnis, 1983; McCleary, 1994). The preponderance of moral thought tends to reject *common knowledge* as a source of truth in favor of vaulted discourse on detached or isolated theoretical propositions. Yet, philosophical theories are built upon conventional ideas that are specific to historical and cultural placement of theoretical development. Moral philosophy cannot stand apart from the conventional knowledge that is used to create it.

Conventional knowledge is the common rationality as applied to human actions within a cultural milieu (Giddens, 1987). As with all other constructs, the study of ethics depends upon conventional *theories* to support its internal integrity and to establish its truth. Moral philosophy is designed to create and to maintain a canon of consistency to be used by philosophers as its narrative tradition. This canon specifies not only what counts as acceptable theory and method, but what conventional knowledge is needed by theory developers.

The canon of moral philosophy is founded in specific assumptions about sources of conduct which are defended and perpetuated as the *truth*. Conventional terms such as morality, utilitarianism, deontological ethics, consequentialist, etc. perpetuates the dominant paradigm by indicating some variation of the conventional ideas used to develop theory. Any deviation from convention must fall within specific boundaries or it is rejected as *untruthful, illogical, contradictory,* or "it just doesn't make sense." Convention is fiercely protected by those who have the greatest interest in its perpetuation, and is substantially modified only by an overwhelming accumulation of evidence that cannot be shouted down by the old paradigm's defenders (Kuhn, 1970).

Convention is an adaptive mechanism that has facilitated stability in human society, and is needed for continuity of thought, communication, and culture. One of Adam's first tasks in the Garden of Eden was to name the animals--to create conventional knowledge. The validity of conventional knowledge is generally established in a circular process by the authorities it creates. This process usually follows these steps: knowledge is created; people acquire knowledge and become experts; experts use the knowledge they possess to invalidate competing knowledge; the invalidation of competing knowledge validates the original knowledge.

Those who act out *morality* (or for that matter, *leadership*) need not fully understand the minutia of convention to be in a position to contribute to its validation and to actively suppress the unconventional. Giddens (1987) used the example of writing a check to demonstrate the possibility of acting within the boundaries and with knowledge of convention without necessarily understanding it completely. One does not need to have an elaborate understanding of the banking system to have and to use a checking account. Further, asked about conventional ideas, actors are rarely able to articulate them; we all know what money is until someone asks us to define it specifically. We all know what morality, or leadership, is until someone asks us to define it specifically.

When one writes a check, one does so within the context of a complex array of concepts about what credit is, what account balance is, and so on. Those who act *morally* do so using concepts of goodness, of justice, of success, of moral reasoning, of goals, of responsibility, and so forth. If someone were to act *morally* with different concepts, such as with a different cultural definition of goodness or of responsibility, then a different moral interpretation would be expected to govern the assessment of action. What makes moral systems different among different cultures generally lies in the structure or constitution of the society itself. In the case of organizations, formal structure is a key element because it is the only feature that distinguishes organizations from other groups of people who occupy definable boundaries and who have common purposes, such as the crowd at a football game.

The relationship between action and structure must be mitigated by what Giddens (1982) called *the duality of structure*. Structural properties of social systems are both medium and outcomes of the practices and activities that comprise those systems. People behave in common ways to produce customs. Customs are organized into moral systems. Moral systems are institutionalized, and influence the way people learn to behave. Conforming behavior validates moral systems, and deviant behavior puts pressure on those systems to change. When the pressure to change is sufficient, the systems are modified along with the conventional ideas that support them. The complex, reciprocal relationships of people and institutions, then, must be the foci of the explanation of moral order.

Giddens (1987) proposed four conditions of convention that have implications for moral behavior. First, a person's conventional view is bounded by a fairly limited cultural milieu within a pluralistic society. We adopt a perceptual universe that is bounded by what we know and by those who agree with what we know. A person's interpretation of conduct, then, is validated only within a narrow social context that naturally suppresses unconventional interpretations.

Second, a given person can identify relatively little about the complex conventional frameworks that structure activities. We live our lives for the most part on automatic pilot, reflecting minimally on why we are doing this or that. The creation of convention and of conventional institutions is one of the ways that we accomplish more with less effort.

We develop standardized solutions to common problems, and apply those solutions automatically. Most people who drive automobiles regularly do not need to contemplate applying the brake when they see a stop sign. By standardizing conceptual thought and custom, we habitualize our social behavior, and reduce the choices needed to carry out our activities and the amount of thought and energy required to act.

Third, actions we take have consequences that we may not be able to predict, and of which we may be oblivious. Convention is as much the result of unintended consequences of action as it is of intended consequences. To illustrate unintended consequences, Giddens used the example of speaking English. When speaking correctly, one usually does not intend to reproduce the structures of the English language, yet that is the outcome. Action taken within a social context necessarily influences all other actions and interpretations of actions.

Fourth, given that all human action occurs within some limits of time and space, we are each influenced by institutions and by social structures that are the outcome of our collective actions, but which none of us has intentionally created. The moral and governing systems which have for millennia been the subject of philosophical speculation are the equivalent of policy created by a committee--all has been created by us collectively, but none is precisely what any one of us thinks it should be. Compromise and adaptation generated by collective input have a norming affect on standards of conduct that produce outcomes which are acceptable but not ideal.

Institutions, in this sense, are more than simply the environment within which human action is taken because they shape the conventions that govern (provide rationale for) conduct. For this reason, leadership can never be completely the result of one person's conduct. Action taken by an individual reconstitutes the conditions for actions of others which reciprocally change the conditions for the original actor. This reciprocation ultimately shapes and reshapes social institutions, and minimizes the role of any single actor in creating outcomes. To expect multiple and continuous manifestations of this process to result in standard or universal moral systems is entirely unreasonable.

Studying Ethics

The conventional view of the relationship between ethics and leadership is a reflection of the conventional view of each respective concept. The conventional view of leadership holds that the individual in the high position is the source of outcomes. The conventional view of ethics holds that the individual person is the source of moral behavior. Together, they can proceed nowhere but to the conclusion that the leader, who is in charge of outcomes, will act morally or not by choice, and that outcomes will necessarily be a result of these choices.

Here-to-fore, the sum total of "ethics in leadership" has amounted to a set of admonishments for the individual in the high position to do the right thing; don't pollute; be good to your employees; don't cheat your customers. The actual result is that most executives and politicians operate right up to the legal boundaries, and do basically whatever they feel they can get away with doing. Ethicists can do little more than appear on network news programs and wag their fingers, complaining that these *leaders* are not following their advice.

In the year 2001, a businessman, convicted of cheating his customers, was ordered by a California judge to take a business ethics course as part of his sentence. This innovation in the delivery of justice has some important implications for that which we call ethics. If the judge was not intending to imply that taking an ethics course is a form of punishment equal to prison, then the operating assumption must have been that studying ethics increases the probability of future moral (or at least legal) behavior. This assumption seems to be shared by virtually all schools that require students to take courses in ethics. Similarly, courses in leadership studies are thought to result in improved leadership abilities in individuals.

In discussing with students who have taken an ethics course what they have learned, one would be hard pressed to account for any changes in thinking or in behavior. Leadership training likewise proceeds with little or no tangible result, primarily because there is no widely accepted definition of leadership with which to compare. Leadership training that includes ethics training must therefore represent the very pinnacle of human folly; we do not know what leadership is and we do not know what ethics are, but we are training ethical leaders for the future.

The fundamental problem for applications of ethics in organizations is that the whole of the subject is poorly defined and scholarship in the area, as in leadership studies, is so obsessed with *experimenta lucifera* that there is little in the way of organized theory for the practitioner, or for that matter for the teacher, to know. The typical text in business ethics begins with a discussion of moral theories, but quickly degenerates into telling stories about specific cases such as Firestone or Exxon and posing the questions for students "is there a moral issue here? What is your opinion?" without any conclusion that is tied directly to narrative traditions in moral philosophy.

Efforts to construct and to teach techniques for resolving *moral dilemmas* serve to illustrate little more than why Socrates felt that dilemmas do not exist for those who know themselves well enough. Perhaps the solution is to frame a *dilemma* as strictly a legal issue. Certainly there are implications to discuss relative to this moral theory or that, but virtually every action taken by an organization can only be interpreted as some form of utilitarianism, and every viable advocation boils down to some issue of legality. There is nothing authors have to offer students that is anything like a theoretical canon, and so we are left with those admonitions: do the right thing; don't pollute; be good to your employees; don't cheat your customers. They have roughly the moral authority of a scolding neighbor. The businessman who received the sentence is likely to have learned more about how to cheat customers legally (because that is his ethic) than about how to be moral.

The *point* in studying anything about organizations is to explain organizational outcomes given that a proper explanation will lead to some degree of predictive control for managers. Most current approaches to understanding organizations have grossly oversimplified the processes involved which result in the outcomes observed; therefore, any given prediction rarely accounts for all the parameters of the problem being addressed. This oversimplification stems partly from turf wars among academics who tend to wall off subjects as though they are some form of personal property, and partly from unexamined assumptions. Complexity generally inspires linear deductive reasoning when a dissipative integration of ideas (sometimes called *bootstrapping*) would be more suitable. Following is an attempt to account for more parameters of social problems than typically are addressed by moral theory.

The Development of Moral Philosophy

The reintroduction of philosophy to the curriculum of higher education in the 13th Century brought with it an assertion that philosophy regarding moral conduct was best formulated and interpreted by *experts*, that is, by academic philosophers and by church-sanctioned authorities. That assertion has been supported by the persistent notion among those authorities that the judgement of right and wrong cannot be entrusted to common people because they lack the appropriate preparation (Bauman, 1994). Industrial leadership theory has extended moral authority to those who occupy high positions, thereby contributing to the conclusion that *leaders* are better than everyone else, and to the inclusion of honesty and other moral dimensions among the leader's traits.

What *experts* represent is *conventional knowledge* about acceptable and unacceptable behavior. Yet in organizations, the rightness or wrongness of action is judged relative to goals and expectations set by managers which necessarily establish the organization's version of conventional knowledge (Barker, 1993; Jackall, 1988). Since most organization members employ moral standards they have learned in society to at least some extent, there is often tension between outside moral standards and inside expectations. Even though managers have been extended moral authority and the assumption of expertise by virtue of their *leadership* positions, they are not usually considered knowledgeable about philosophy and therefore rarely cited personally for orchestrating moral violations unless some degree of central control or responsibility is attributed to them. In other words, actual collusion in wrongdoing means less than a perception of control and responsibility.

In the industrial era, organizations have created untenable problems for moral experts by becoming bothersome illustrations of the dynamic social processes that defy attempts to apply traditional moral theory and detached philosophical wisdom.   Kaufman (1973) observed that bureaucratic managers often privately approve of behavior that they acknowledge publically as illegal or unethical. Expectations for loyalty to the organization and for obedience to managerial direction set the a priori guidelines for moral conduct, and a given organization can develop and impose its own form of influence on the individual with an organizationally specific moral order that can seem to preempt external social order. Organization members can defy common social or religious morality when they are acting on behalf of the organization and feel justified in doing so because their behavior is judged within the context of the organization (Jackall, 1988).   People will act in socially unacceptable ways while inside the organization's boundaries if those actions are consistent with organizational standards and rewarded as such. Society holds the organization accountable as a rational actor, but seldom are the individuals actually responsible for creating organizational outcomes entailed in that accountability.

Modern understanding of ethics emphasizes the behavioral aspects to the extent that the words *ethics* and *morals* are commonly used interchangeably by philosophers to refer to behavioral standards, codes of conduct, or principles upon which these standards and codes are based.

But, the different words imply different things. According to Bauman (1994), "ethics is something more than a mere description of what people do; more even than a description of what they believe they ought to be doing in order to be decent, just, good--or, more generally, 'in the right'" (p. 1).

In ancient times, that which we call ethics was primarily concerned with the right way to live (Boyce, 1979; Durant, 1933; Ferm, 1965). Modern studies of tribal systems have indicated that morality in those societies is often rooted in religion (e.g. Benedict, 1934). Tribal religion may or may not specify rules to follow that are detached from the tribe's system of governance, but religion in tribal societies is designed to provide explanations of the unknown and recipes for living successfully according to some cultural understanding of *our telos*--our ultimate end or purpose. According to Aristotle (1962), the motivation for pursuing this *telos* is that doing so is the only way to bring about *eudaimonia*. *Eudaimonia*, for purposes of this discussion, is defined as the enjoyment and fulfillment one experiences when doing something presumed to be of *consequence*. The *consequence* is important to the extent that it is aligned with one's personal understanding of *telos*. Behavior generated by *telos* is not aimed at an end goal necessarily, but at an abstract *value* that may never be fully realized--the *point*.

For the majority of ancient Greeks, there was no unifying theological source for moral behavior. Bold and virtuous action was good in and of itself, so striving for *eudaimonia* was a function of the individual. After early Christians adapted stoic thought on the subject to their purposes, official *telos* of the Christian world became serving God, and moral behavior was defined accordingly--*telos* and morality were thought to be specific and universal. The problem of right conduct now included some idea of obtaining salvation as an end, and following God's universal rules to avoid sin became the most widely accepted solution.

While serving God is a simple and pragmatic avenue toward the moral life for many Christians, Muslims, and Jews, there are a number of issues regarding the relationship between the free will and an omnipotent God that complicate the philosophical problems of conduct within the realm of these religions. There are further problems manifested in the idea that the organization of the Church represents God. For example, one may commit any sort of crimes and sins against others in the name of the church and be forgiven by a priest who speaks for God. Leaders of all Western religions, in recent times, have encouraged or tolerated socially unacceptable behavior among the members of their congregations that these same leaders condemn in everyone else. The organization of the Church has the same characteristics, issues, and limitations as any other human organization. What happens within the organization is judged by a different standard than the one applied to general society.

The nature of these problems is widely known among theologians and need not be rehearsed here. It is enough to say that many self-contradictions built into Western theology have made development of moral thought beyond natural law difficult if not impossible for believers to abide. Application of natural law is inconsistent among believers, and infeasible in the organization of the Church or any other organization. The simple answers to problems of conduct provided by natural law will never succeed in a precise application to the modern world except to the believer who is willing to deny the tenets of industrial society.

Over time, Christianity, as practiced in Europe, imposed a form of judgement on behavior that measured morality in terms of serving God, which precluded any serious consideration of the meaning of life beyond serving God. Life previously judged by quality was now judged by content. By the time industrial society dominated the Western world, success as defined by *eudaimonia*, even success defined by service to God, had been supplanted by a concept of success defined as a function of measurable achievement and productivity.

Theology encompassed by a tribal *telos* is not necessarily an organized construct of God, of God's domain, and of God's law, but rather it is more of a shared understanding of that which is the source of all things, and of that which gives meaning to life and to existence. Aristotle implied that *eudaimonia* is the fundamental source (as in *final cause*) of noble or virtuous behavior--the foundation of moral choices, of preferential relationships, and of the motivation to act morally. It should be clear that any question of conduct cannot be sufficiently addressed without first having defined that which energizes and sustains behavior--human motivation. Aristotle addressed the issue of motivation in the first line of the *Metaphysics*: "All men by nature desire to know;" and, again, in the first line of *Nicomachean Ethics*: "Every art and every scientific enquiry, and similarly every action and purpose, may be said to aim at some good."

Although the words are commonly used interchangeably, ethics and morals can be thought of as two different but related things. Some authors acknowledge that the two words provide different connotations, but elect not to distinguish between them in discussion (e.g. Runkle, 1982). The word *ethic*, from the Greek word *ethos*, refers to one's character. As Wittgenstein (1958) suggested, "ethics is like aesthetics" (p. 226). Character is often thought to be defined by one's habitual behavior, hence the association of ethics and behavior. The word *moral*, based in the Latin word *mos*, can be understood as custom, which can easily be equated with habitual behavior. Ultimately however, character (ethics) is defined culturally relative to *value*, and not behaviorally.

Morals are the rules or customs; *ethics* represent the character, spirit, or sensibility that facilitates and activates habitual or customary behavior. This interpretation is consistent with the view of ethics as matters of virtue proposed by Aristotle (1961). While Aristotle asserted that virtue is something habitual, he specifically avoided the degree of precision that would be needed to devise specific rules or customs for an individual to follow in defining ethics behaviorally (Duska, 1993). Ethics are concerned with the manifestation of the Good in each person, and the manifestation of the Good can be measured by *eudaimonia*. The rules and customs were, for Aristotle, a matter of politics.

Ethics specify the nature of *consequence* needed for the experience of joy and contentment to occur. *Consequence* emanates through cultural perceptions of reality upon which choices of action are made. Ethics embody a fundamental life orientation (*telos*) that answers the question "what is life's greatest good?" or *summum bonum* for the individual. Ethics are not collective in the sense that morals are collective; ethics may be shared, but they are not necessarily dependent upon the approval of others. The question of external approval will be addressed in greater detail later.

Morals are, by contrast, subject to the approval of others. Ethics may be considered an individual's spiritual definition of life--that purpose for which life is intended. A person's ethic is descended from a world view--a set of assumptions, associated values, and object moral principles which manifest themselves in a characteristic pattern of decisions that presuppose moral outcomes. These decisions are the source of moral behavior that can be assessed relative to virtue, and that answers the question "what sort of behavior is required to bring about life's greatest good?" for each individual or for a group of associated individuals. The reward for moral behavior that is consistent with an ethic is *eudaimonia*.

Ethics are not judgements; judgements are actions, and therefore part of a moral system (Nietzsche, 1974, 4:335). Nietzsche maintained that judgements can be made immorally, and therefore are subject to the same rules as other behaviors. Ethics represent an individual's take on the broad, socially constructed reality assimilated as an outcome of socialization into a *culture*. Morals are sets of rules and principles for rule following that are based in a conventional method of reasoning.

An ethic can be understood as a source of behavior that originates from within a socially constructed reality, where basic ontological assumptions, culturally specific emotions, and socially derived values serve as forceful guidelines for the creation of conscious moral systems in conjunction with personal insight and experience. Different individuals may experience different degrees of awareness of their ethics, of the mores that influence their ethics, or of the relationship between their conscious processes and their subconscious subroutines of behavior. Social mores manifest themselves within individuals through the socialization process, and the nature of that manifestation emerges when the individual acts. This action may conflict with the individual's explanation of it because its source may be entirely obscure to the individual. An ethic is a manifestation of a moral order that is largely subconscious, but profoundly compelling. Ethics are open to conscious exploration, analysis, and modification through experience and reflective thought, even though most of us feel compelled to behave correctly with little reflection on why.

The reciprocal relationship between ethics and morals can be summed thus: An ethic is an individual's take on conventional knowledge about purpose and goodness (*telos*) that results from *socialization* into the culture. Morals are rules and principles of behavior that people follow or not in carrying out their ethics. Individual ethics can be modified through reflection and experience. Individuals learn moral systems, but can adapt them to given contexts and situations. Adaptation of behavior is guided by ethics. If an individual's behavior deviates from conventional moral standards, pressure is brought to bear upon the individual to conform, but also upon the mores behind those standards. Sufficient pressure on mores stimulates a restructuring in the moral order, and the resulting modifications are assimilated by individuals.

A Case For Relativism

The common criticism of moral relativism is that if it were true everyone would be free to do anything and justify it by saying "it's all relative." That would be the case only if one defines morality as a function of the individual, and if one assumes that justification is the source of behavior. If morality is established by the moral order of a society, then all societies can have immoral individuals, but a moral action in one society can possibly be an immoral action in another society. Moral relativism is considered by many to be a legitimate method of explaining the diversity of moral theories in different cultures. To others, moral relativism is inappropriate and fails to prove that there is no true or superior (absolute) moral system (Bloom, 1987; Rachels, 1986).

Following are typical arguments against using moral relativism (Shaw & Barry, 2001): First, moral practices of one culture cannot be legitimately criticized by people from another culture because the systems are relative to each respective culture. Second, there can be no such thing as moral progress, which must be judged by an absolute standard. Third, members of a given society cannot legitimately criticize the moral standards accepted by their own society because there is no absolute standard to use as the basis for argument.

These arguments against moral relativism begin with the rather ethnocentric assumption that there is only one form of moral system. There are at least three forms of morality that can be distinguished on the basis of their origins. Each of these three forms can be incorporated to various degrees into a single moral system. First, all moral systems contain a subset of standards that are established by basic, fundamental human needs that all humans experience. These particular standards-- such as prohibitions against murder, rape, assault, incest, stealing, etc.-- appear to be universal because of what all people have in common with each other, such as the desire to live and thrive without being molested.

Second, moral systems usually contain a subset of standards that are developed to address what can broadly be called *environmental conditions*. These standards confront issues arising from the interaction between people and the circumstances of their environment. For example, all societies have accepted moral standards relating to the production, distribution, and consumption of food because food is needed by all people. However, standards related to the type of food consumed, such as restrictions on meat or shellfish, can be based in environmental variables. Under certain environmental conditions, infanticide has made sense to *reasonable* members of a society. Environmental conditions are likely to influence moral standards regarding marriage, birth control, and capital punishment. The need for capital punishment is less obvious to members of a society who have the means to contain and to control enemies (or competitors) easily.

Third, moral systems also usually contain a subset of standards that are established according to conventional knowledge regarding social control--conventional knowledge which is used to define and to solve specific social problems. These control standards are not inspired by the human condition as much as by a complex interaction between the social contract (the social construct of governance) and the individual's desire to act on natural impulses of love, hate, jealousy, greed, lust, and ambition in some conventional way. These are the standards that are likely to vary from society to society, or from organization to organization, primarily because different social entities have different conventional ideas about what constitutes a social problem. In an organization, a social problem can mean poor quality, micromanagement, theft, domination by one department, cost inefficiency, inappropriate structure, labor/management strife, corporate image, loss of market share, and so on.

Criticism of one society's moral standards by another is commonly based either in a misunderstanding of environmental conditions, or in some disagreement with definitions of social problems and how to solve them. Moral progress is itself judged solely within a context of conditions and control, and fairly judged only by those who understand those conditions. If environmental conditions change, what constitutes moral progress must be redefined. When individuals criticize the accepted practices of their own society, the criticism is usually directed at elements of the moral system that provide for control of resources and for the distribution of power--disagreements regarding conventional approaches to solving social problems. Rarely does any member of a given society openly advocate theft, rape, murder, or any change to standards associated with the first form. None of the common criticisms invalidates the concept of moral relativism, even though moral standards that appear to be universal may still exist.

The Psychology of Ethics

A case can be made that a cultural *telos* was represented for Hellenic people by the Good. If that were true, any real understanding of that possibility was lost in the great disaster described by MacIntyre (1984), and we are left with Aristotle's version of the Good, as that at which all things aim, without much in the way of theological implications.

Alasdair MacIntyre, has suggested that we have suffered a great disaster in moral philosophy and do not even realize it. According to MacIntyre, ethics, which was first proposed as a study by Aristotle, was ignored and forgotten through the Middle Ages because of the growth of Christianity. By the time the study of ethics was revived during the Age of Enlightenment, people had largely forgotten what ethics really were, and all they possessed were fragments of a conceptual scheme consisting mostly of language and a body of knowledge that contains bits and pieces of theory. The revival of the study of ethics pulled the fragments and the language together into a set of practices. So philosophers have been arguing over the relative merits of theories, the full meaning and context of which have been forgotten. Adherence to these theory fragments has taken on a ritualistic character where the players conform to the canons of consistency and coherence, but the context needed to make sense of all this has been lost. As a result, the language of ethics which is being used to argue opposing notions of truth is in a "grave state of disorder", undetectable by analytical, by phenomenological, or by existential philosophy.

MacIntyre felt that philosophical analysis will not help us sort things out. Only history may be used to understand the disordered state, although even history cannot be considered objective and neutral. To us, history appears to be a progression of moral philosophy, one philosophy succeeding another. The language of academic history is less than two centuries old, and has been developed under the same disastrous conditions. Therefore, as also implied by Tolstoy, the language of history cannot provide the means to enlighten the academic community as to the fate of the real world. In fact, the current forms of academic curriculum are among the symptoms of the disaster. The language of morality, according to MacIntyre, is unusable in its present state.

Theology encompassed by a tribal *telos* is a shared understanding of that which is the source of all things, and of that which gives meaning to life and to existence--that which creates *value* (Pirsig's idea of *value* as discussed in Chapter 1). *Value* is understood beyond its role as a component of preferential relationships to be the source of those relationships. For ethics, choices are made upon a foundation of *value*.

Motivation is thought by most motivation theorists to be internally generated by needs. If motivation is indeed the result of internally experienced needs, then motivation is born of deprivation. One does not need something unless one has been deprived of it; if you do not need food, it is because you have recently eaten. Most traditional moral theories have incorporated this view of motivation--need for pleasure, need for tranquility, need for salvation. By understanding value as the source of *needs*, motivation models such as Maslow's difficult to apply hierarchy become immediately more comprehensive, and deviations from the structure of the hierarchy can be more readily explained.

It is beyond the scope of this discussion to create a new theory of motivation, or to specifically address any of the existing theories. However, anyone familiar with thought on motivation can understand the possibilities for the idea that at least some motivational forces are generated by deep seated, persistent values that are experienced at both instinctual and cognitive levels before any assessment of needs can take place. Someone sitting on a hot stove does not contemplate the *need* to jump off the hot stove before experiencing the motivation to do so; an engineer may not contemplate the *need* to solve a problem before experiencing the motivation to do so. The values in question are not abstract intellectual or religious constructs, but fundamental attractions such as the value a sunflower has for the sun.

Moral theories must necessarily begin with some theory of psychology. Either people act through conscious choices, or they are subject to overwhelming subconscious impulses, or they are simply programmable components in a great mechanistic contingency schedule. In any case, moral choices originate in some form of cognitive behavior the origins of which must be explained before any application of reasoning or assessment of responsibility can begin. One limitation for modern moral philosophy has been the failure of psychologists to agree upon an adequate model of the origins of cognitive processes. Even though moral philosophers have not been clamoring for a better model, a promising construct has been developed by Harré, Clark, and DeCarlo (1985).

Conventional constructs of psychology (excluding behaviorism) tend to classify the sources of individual behavior into a two tier model. The lower tier is thought to be predominated by subconscious impulses that are potentially subject to control by the higher tier--consciously directed behavior. It is normally assumed that the individual is entirely capable of consciously choosing a moral system from those offered by society and the extent to which that system is followed. Defined only within this framework, ethics must necessarily be understood as consciously developed systems of control. In this case, ethics (the control systems) and morals (the principles of control upon which the systems are based) could be perceived as two interdependent elements of the same thing. Harré et al. have proposed a three tier construct: (a) the first tier is predominated by subconscious subroutines of behavior that are used to execute plans and to govern standard conduct, (b) the conscious rule systems referred to above comprise the second tier, and (c) the third tier is the subconscious influence of conventional social or collective processes and structures of multiple and potentially varied moral orders.

The first tier can be represented by any given routine that is consciously learned and then committed to the subconscious for the purpose of carrying out plans: like a golf swing, eating in public, or the routine one sets into motion upon arising in the morning. The second tier is governed by conscious moral theories and by rational behavior, but in this model it is less the strategic controller of behavior and more the middle manager, converting direction to action. The second tier links the influence of cultural convention contained in the third tier with the individual's behavioral subroutines in the first tier. The third tier is a deep structure in the mind that provides a framework within which conventional knowledge is ordered and conscious action is initiated. Conventional explanations of reality, cultural theories of conduct and self-management, definitions of social problems and how to solve them, an understanding of obligations and responsibilities, and concepts of social roles and relationships are all contained in the third tier. While the third tier represents a strong influence on behavior, its influence operates outside of the awareness of most people.

Within this model, an ethic can be understood as a source of behavior that originates from within a socially constructed reality, where basic ontological assumptions, culturally specific emotions, and socially derived values serve as forceful guidelines for the creation of conscious moral systems in conjunction with personal insight and experience. Different individuals may experience different degrees of awareness of their ethics, the mores that influence their ethics, or the relationship between their conscious processes and their subconscious subroutines. Social mores manifest themselves within individuals through the socialization process, and the character of that manifestation emerges when the individual acts. An action may conflict with the individual's explanation of it if the subroutines carried out by the individual are inconsistent with the content of the consciousness.

The deep seated, persistent *value* that precedes an individual's assessment of needs is the substance of the third tier. Because this *value* is the biological and cognitive *substance* of the individual, it is the source of all that constitutes the individual's personality or character, physiologically or psychologically. An ethic is a manifestation of a moral order that is largely subconscious, but profoundly compelling, ordered within the individual by deep, structural *value*.

Ethics are open to conscious exploration, analysis, and modification through experience and reflective thought, and can be modified extensively given the will and the capacity of the individual to do so. Human beings are not simply the hapless recipients of culture, they have the inherent ability to override social influences on their behavior (Handy, 1993; Opler, 1964). On the other hand, most of us feel compelled to behave correctly, and not compelled to make profound changes. Inconsistencies between behavior and the rationale for that behavior can result from conscious adoption of changes in social mores without corresponding modifications either in subroutines, or in third tier structures, or in both. Inconsistencies can also result from unsystematic or incomplete assimilation of culture, or from physiological sources.

Morality in an Industrial Society

The framework of ontological assumptions about ethics and morals in any given society is hidden to the practitioner's eye by a facade of convention. Conventional knowledge provides the means for us to carry out our daily lives and to establish and maintain our institutions, but it allows us to act in accordance with its principles without having profound knowledge of its sources. Whenever one obeys traffic rules, whenever one follows a boss's instructions, or whenever one takes any such action, institutional needs are both served and reinforced without the actor's specific intent (Giddens, 1982).

In an industrial society, moral systems must accommodate certain environmental and social control conditions. First, some provision must be made to accommodate exploitation. An industrial economy cannot work unless a majority of workers are coerced into working hard to make someone else rich. Moral theory must account for this condition. Since most workers perform tasks that they would never choose to do on their own, they must be made to feel morally compelled to do so. To industrial leadership scholars, this is the central problem that leadership must solve.

Initially this problem was solved by John Calvin, who made tedious work a symptom of salvation. As the Calvinistic work ethic waned, it was supplanted by theories of loyalty and justice. One does this work out of obligation to the employer, or in the case of Marxism obligation to the proletariate, or simply to get one's fair share of industrial output. Under conventional theories of justice, a low level worker can agree that her or his share is necessarily and fairly less than that of the business owner. Under Marxism, those who benefit the most from industrial output must maintain the perception in others that they receive much less than they actually do.

Second, moral theory in industrial society must accommodate, if not institutionalize, greed, which is to say material consumerism. The fundamental mechanism of a market economy is greed--it provides the energy that runs the system, both greed for capital gain and greed for consumable products. The modern moral theorist must assimilate the natural human parameters of greed that have been incorporated into industrial society and promote property rights on the same level as human need in order to accommodate those who are in control of resources.

John Locke (1947) anticipated the problems of greed and exploitation by declaring that property is not simply a possession, but a key source of identity for the individual because it represents the only real compensation for allowing oneself to be exploited--I worked hard for this, doing work I dislike, so now it's mine and I deserve it. If a person's identity is at least partially defined by what he or she possesses, then property rights become more than just legal issues; they become moral issues--injury to property is injury to self.

The adaptation of morality to industrial society has been less the task of moral theory than of theories of justice. Nozick (1974) argued that people have a basic moral right to pursue their own ends without interference, and that they are *entitled* to property acquired fairly. This idea can be separated from basic hedonism by its context, that is by industrial capitalism. Rawls (1971) suggested that persons in the *original position* would agree on two things: that certain fundamental liberties are guaranteed to each person, and that social and economic inequalities are justified if they are designed to benefit the least advantaged members of society.

Because there is no reasonable expectation that those in power will give up their power to the disadvantaged, ideas are designed to validate long-held conventional wisdom regarding the superiority of some members of society over others, and the moral rights of these members to exploit others for their own personal gain. The right to exploit and to coerce others is justified by an espoused commitment to civil rights and to affirmative action, and by an articulated compassion for the condition of the exploited. Capitalism requires continuous growth for its existence, therefore the moral bottom line for industrial society is *productivity*. Virtually any conduct can be justified if it ultimately results in an increase in productivity. Leadership is understood by industrial theorists as a tool for achieving productivity through the exploitation of others.

The Eudaimonic Form of Life

Defining ethics and distinguishing ethics from morals does not address the *point* of conducting such an exercise in the first place. Of central importance to the study of leadership--to an understanding of the engine of leadership--is the following question: What motivates people to take specific and directed action to bring about certain outcomes? *Eudaimonia* has been suggested as a possible answer, and that answer warrants further consideration because it suggests that people participate in leadership as a means to live the good life.

Aristotle arrived at his understanding of *eudaimonia* by addressing the following question: Why does anyone do anything? The answer to why a person does this or that begins with "because..." and may require subsequent answers. Why do you go to college? Because I want to get a good job. Why do you want a good job? Because I want to make money. Why... etc. Answering with "because" cannot go on forever; eventually one will come to the final "because" which cannot be clarified further. That final "because" is what Aristotle called *eudaimonia*. *Eudaimonia* is that for the sake of which we do everything. There are many qualifications to this idea that need not be restated in this discussion. Here we shall consider that part of the development which will help us to understand leadership.

Eudaimonia has been defined in this discussion as the enjoyment and fulfillment one experiences when doing something presumed to be of *consequence*. This definition should not be taken as Aristotle's specific view, but rather as one interpretation of his view, somewhat modified. First, *eudaimonia* is experienced in harmony with one's true nature--one's ethic. In other words, *eudaimonia* is experienced while involved in the sort of activity that defines the nature of the person who is acting. One will not experience *eudaimonia* when engaged in forced moral behavior that is inconsistent with one's ethic--as in "alright, I'll do the right thing, dammit."

Aristotle maintained that all humans are defined by rational thought. No doubt, Aristotle had the Hellenic version of rational thought in mind, so allowances must be made for individual and cultural differences regarding what constitutes rational thought. Aristotle would not allow, for example, that members of organized crime can live an *eudaimonic* form of life. But here, that will be considered a possibility if the mafia has met conditions, which will be discussed later, for constituting a political community. In this discussion, individuals are assumed to be defined by what is often called *personality*. Personality is a very complex idea used to describe that structure of a person's behavior and sources of behavior that is created, maintained, and displayed through social interaction. Personality is a function of culture. If there were only one person in the world, that person would have no recognizable personality nor any means to develop one. Personality is formulated out of the learning and practice of social roles and the expectations and responsibilities that accompany those roles. Leadership is, itself, supposed to be a process of definition or of redefinition; one indicator that leadership is being experienced is an affect on personality.

Second, *eudaimonia* is not a peak experience; it is not something only experienced occasionally; nor is it something experienced randomly. *Eudaimonia* is created from an habitual pattern of action that is formed out of social learning. This pattern of action is both deliberate and sustained. It is an ordered and carefully considered pattern that has *consequence* in the sense that it is carried out for the sake of something greater than the self.

Eudaimonia is harmony--as in an harmonic relationship. This harmonic relationship exists between the nature of the person (that person's ethic) and moral behavior. Just as the notes of C and G played together represent an harmonic relationship, so the notes C# and G# represent that same harmonic relationship in a different key. When the notes are no longer sounding--interrupted or ceased--harmony disappears. When deliberate and sustain activity of *consequence* ceases, *eudaimonia* disappears. A musical melody is a set of harmonic relationships which remain intact when played in a different key. The harmonic relationships of behavior and ethic that produce *eudaimonia* remain intact when played out according to a different cultural standard. Different notes, same harmony; different behavior, same *eudaimonia*. The opposite of harmony would be dissonance. The harmonic relationship that creates *eudaimonia* does not preclude the existence of conflict with outside forces or with other people, but it does suggest a form of purity created by the absence of dissonance.

Aristotle specified two possibilities for creating the experience of *eudaimonia*, but did not leave the impression that he favored one over the other. The first possibility is the life of contemplation. The second possibility is the life of participation in civic and political affairs. Aristotle was quite clear that neither of these possibilities is available to everyone. *Eudaimonia* can only be experienced by those who are properly prepared for the experience. People with an underdeveloped, incomplete, or corrupted character could not possibly experience *eudaimonia* or understand what it means. Underdeveloped character is like a piano with only six notes. Incomplete character is like an eighty eight key piano that has some number of keys which make no sound when struck. Corrupted character is like a piano that is out of tune. To the observation that unprepared students rarely change their behavior as a result of taking ethics courses, Aristotle would reply "of course they wouldn't, how could you expect them to?"

Eudaimonia is a form of pleasure, but it should not be regarded in the same company with other pleasures. Sexual orgasm is pleasure; conversation can be pleasure; watching something entertaining is pleasure; relaxing is pleasure. But, none of these pleasures approach what is here called *eudaimonia*, which is thought to be a higher quality of pleasure. Aristotle, and others who have addressed the topic, have tended to restrict the experience of *eudaimonia* to a person of virtue or of superior intellect, and this restriction can be criticized as elitist.

John Stuart Mill (1910), arguing in favor of the qualitative nature of pleasure, suggested that it is indisputable that some beings' capacity for enjoyment is low. "It is better to be a human being dissatisfied than a pig satisfied; better to be Socrates dissatisfied than a fool satisfied. And if the fool, or the pig, are of a different opinion, it is because they only know their own side of the question. The other party to the comparison knows both sides" (p. 9). How could one party know both sides? Given that Mill was neither a fool nor a pig, how could he possibly know *their* side of the question? How could Mill, or anyone else for the matter, know what Socrates experienced? That is the problem of elitism--attribution of one's own experience to others under the assumption of superiority of mind.

While it makes sense to accept the notion that underdeveloped, incomplete, and corrupted individuals are incapable of experiencing *eudaimonia*, it does not follow that the experience is only open to the wealthy, the learned, the ambitious, and the powerful. When an individual pursues an activity that is judged by that individual to be of *consequence* according to an ethic, no other person may judge the authenticity of that experience. What another person may judge is the outcome or intended outcome relative to some conventional standard of contribution. No one may assume mastery of the moral order or any complete comprehension of it.

The experience of *eudaimonia* is governed by convention to the extent that an individual's ethic is founded in conventional moral order.

If there were no moral order, there would be no grounds for the judgement of good and bad. If there were only one person on earth, that person would have no basis for categorizing even the basic experiences of pleasure and pain. Convention is the manner in which we standardize our ethics and communicate them to others, and convention is the tool we use for developing *personality*. A personality is just that collection of roles, role expectations, standards, and ideals learned from the moral order that provides the basis for deciding upon the actions and directions of one's life. A personality is that by which the ideal lives lived by saints can be appreciated and aspired to. Convention finds its place in the individual's assessment of *consequence* because that is the source of the standards and ideals of summum bonum.

When Aristotle (1969) explored the various forms of friendship, he concluded that the most meaningful friendship was created out of choices made and action taken by an individual according to the express benefit of the other. This conclusion was a natural extension of his view of the nature of *eudaimonia* and the requisite virtue needed for its experience. An *eudaimonic* form of life is a life lived for the sake of others, and cannot be experienced by someone whose joy is restricted to activities that have nothing more than self-gratification as their goal. Playing video games, running marathons, watching sports, betting on the stock market, or sitting alone listening to music will not produce *eudaimonia*. Playing video games with friends, rooting for the home team, belonging to an investment club, or listening to live music in a concert hall as part of an habitual scheme of activity could very possibly be elements of an *eudaimonic* form of life if carried out for the sake of something outside the self. Risking contradiction with Aristotle, I would maintain that someone living a life of contemplation who does not share that contemplation with others is not living an *eudaimonic* form of life.

Though Aristotle would probably not agree, I take the position that activities that stimulate meaningful interaction among people toward a shared value can be experienced as having *consequence*. Having derived one's personality through interaction with others, one then seeks communication from others that indicates when one is on the right track. It is the process of seeking communication that probably generates, or not, the sensation of *consequence*. *Consequence* can only be defined in relation to the communication one receives from others. It is possible that contradiction is the *consequence* one is seeking, but the process remains the same. It is this process of devising *consequence*, of seeking to improve the state of others for their own sake, that creates social organization, and that becomes the basis for a political community. Pursuit of this form of *consequence* is the heart of the leadership process, and is in place as a catalyst for social development. People are constituted in this way that they might choose difficult and painful paths for the sake of others. And, why not? Given that your personality is a function of everyone else, to serve others is literally to serve yourself.

Fulfillment gained in seeking out and improving the state of others should not necessarily be interpreted as pleasure. It might be a deep and abiding sense of satisfaction. A *eudaimonic* form of life is a process that can include many instances of frustration and anxiety. Aristotle correctly maintained that the experience of *eudaimonia* is not available to all people, just as the experience of the complete friendship is not possible for all people. One who is self-oriented may experience pleasure, but will not experience *eudaimonia*. One who is only occasionally concerned with the well being of others will not experience *eudaimonia*. One who merely provides socially acceptable rationale for behavior and moral choices will not experience *eudaimonia*.

The *eudaimonic* form of life is an approach to living that is not self-conscious; it is not simply a set of motives, activities, or prescriptions for behavior given certain conditions. It is a form of life that, once established, is self-perpetuating, self-energizing, and self-validating. It is not bestowed nor is it achieved. It represents a life devoted to discovering and to meeting the needs of others simply because those needs exist and because the actor is in a position to meet them. It is not a life of seeking glory or recognition. If you are contemplating setting out to achieve *eudaimonia*, save your bus fare, you have already failed.

What is bestowed is a perception of authenticity judged according to conventional standards and ideals set by the moral order. The *authentic life* is something that must be ultimately judged by others. Herodotus, the famous ancient historian, suggested that such a life can be judged only after it has been lived, and has nothing to do with amassing wealth and power or with gaining high position and notoriety. In other words, an *authentic life* is a life measured against conventional ideals and standards as applied to the qualitative aspect of life rather than to the material aspect. It is a life understood as above and beyond the level of average which observers would choose to live themselves if not for their acknowledged mediocrity--their weaknesses, foolishness, and selfishness. *Authenticity* is a collective judgement of contribution, and not of status. A life can only be called *authentic* if it is an example of a cultural archetype such that it can be pointed out to illustrate cultural ideals--those ideals used to define *contribution* to the culture and to society. Herodotus maintained that wealth, power, and majesty do not represent the sort of ideals that define an archetype of "the happiest of men."

To argue that a life must be completed in order for its authenticity-- its value relative to conventional ideals--to be assessed is to allow that convention may change over time, and that the ideals in question are enduring rather than faddish elements of the moral order. Further, that argument is an admonishment to consider only nonmaterial ideals--to measure success according to contribution and not according to achievement. Long after his death, the life of Francis of Assisi is celebrated by people who could not name one king who ruled during his lifetime. The *authentic life* is a life of habitually asking what needs to be done, and habitually doing what is indicated as an answer. It is not a life lived while consciously seeking approval. The life of civic affairs--asking only what one can do for one's country--is probably what Aristotle had in mind as a *eudaimonic* form of life.

The Role of Ethics In Leadership

The engine of leadership is powered by the energy derived from some number of individuals experiencing the joy and contentment of doing something of *consequence*. Joy is not simply pure pleasure, but it is the sensation of spiritual growth derived from habitually doing the right thing for the sake of others. Contentment is not satisfaction with the status quo, but contentment that actions taken will have *consequence* for the world in some meaningful way. Within this process, there will be individuals recognizable for their embodiment of conventional ideals. There will also be individuals who are not recognized for their embodiment of ideals.

The engine of leadership is fueled by the energy of a *telos* which is converted in the black box to action taken in accordance with the wants and needs of all those concerned. It is unreasonable to assume that there is a clear consensus on what should be done and why, and it is fair to assume that some degree of conflict over resources and control is present in this engine. The limitations of a mechanistic model now become apparent. Normally when there is noise in a system, it loses power (gains entropy). It will be argued in later chapters that the engine of leadership exchanges energy with its environment and can actually be energized under conditions that would cause a mechanical system to stop functioning. The engine is a sum total of individual wills, individuals whose ethics are potentially compatible if not already in alignment. These individuals possess some degree of understanding relative to the needs of others in the social group and to their common goals, and are prepared to act in accordance with that understanding. Their efforts may be both increased and aligned by various sources of energy from both inside and outside the system.

Some individuals involved in the process are motivated by habitual consideration for the well being of others, and some are more self-oriented. Some are seeking only to serve; others are seeking elevation. All individuals involved in the process recognize, at some level, that conventional understandings or institutions are not working and require of some degree of adjustment. If they did not recognize the need for change, there would be no incentive to act in any but a conventional way.

Chapter 3

The Vessel of Leadership

A vessel is a container. One limitation of the analogy of the ship is that it implies a neatly configured package within which leadership is contained. While the analogy of the ship is useful, it does not represent the whole story. Another vessel analogy that will be suggested in later pages is that of a river bed. The primary difference between these two containers has to do with relativity of movement. In the analogy of the ship, leadership and its vessel are understood to move together, and leadership is stationary relative to its container. In the analogy of the river bed, leadership moves through its vessel, and containment requires a different understanding. Neither of these analogies is a perfect fit, and the reality probably lies somewhere in between. In the following discussion, very little effort will be expended attempting to determine the proper assignment of each element to one of the two analogies under the assumption that such assignment would probably be an oversimplification anyway. Still, the analogies are useful in portraying a very complex idea.

If one word must be used to describe the vessel of leadership, that word must be *organization*. Certainly in industrial society, chartered organizations are entities that are inextricably linked to all other social institutions. It would be a mistake, however, to limit our thinking to the sort of hierarchical organization represented by businesses, clubs, churches, charities, and governments. The *organization* that is the vessel of leadership is a social structure with more or less recognizable boundaries that contain a group of people who have more or less similar wants and needs. This structure is usually more like a network than it is like a pyramid. To understand the relationship of social organization to leadership, adjustments must be applied to certain academic fads and other cherished prejudices.

Organizations Do Not Have Cultures

The concept of *culture* has been applied to organizational studies for some decades. Schein (1992) has gone as far as to suggest that the only thing leaders do of importance is to create and to manage culture. Whatever it is in organizations that is managed is not *culture*. Organizations are created out of *culture* and not vise versa. Implying that *culture* can be managed by one person or by some group of persons is alone sufficient reason for dismissing the concept of organizational culture altogether.

As an early enthusiast for this approach, I have used this form of explanation to a degree as great as anyone, and have so stated (Barker, 1994). I am now of the conviction that the present construct of organizational culture, while useful in some respects, is less than a comprehensive, or even adequate, explanation of organizational outcomes. The argument for this conviction will be slight, and developed only to the extent that it contributes to the *point* of studying leadership. An alternative to the concept of culture as a method of explanation will be presented later in this chapter, and its value for supplanting or for augmenting the notion of organizational culture will be left to the reader's judgement.

The first problem with the concept of culture as applied to organizations is purely ontological; there has been no supportable argument that organizational culture really exists. The ontological issues related to social culture have not even been fully settled among anthropologists. The concept of organizational culture, for the most part, is based on an extrapolation of the dialectical materialism used in the formation of certain anthropological theory. Rather than a more or less natural process of social evolution affecting the *culture* of the dialectical materialists, the development of organizational culture is thought to be governed by strategic management and by the application of progressive rational thought.

The existence of organizational culture is assumed to be established through measurement of organizational variables (e.g. Hofstede, 1980). Having measurable variables implies that something real is being measured, but it does not follow that what is being measured is *culture* just because the measurer claims it is. In fact, Hofstede's work has been criticized in that he failed to establish that even nations have distinctive cultures (McSweeney, 2002).

Culture in society can be granted ontological standing by virtue of the profound, observable differences between social groups. For example, language is a cultural artifact that is often used to establish cultural differences. The differences among organizational languages are usually represented by the use of jargon, acronyms, and words with special meaning, not the structural and linguistic differences one finds by a comparison of Chinese and English. If one English speaking organization uses engineering jargon and another uses accounting jargon, it does not represent the sort of differences one observes between Chinese people and English people. One may conclude that a Chinese speaking organization has a different culture than an English speaking organization, but it is strictly a social distinction and not an organizational phenomenon.

The concept of *culture* has been developed around the idea of social institutions and their influence in the outcomes of human life which can be empirically confirmed. For example, the institution of religion and the institution of marriage can both be defining factors in social culture. While organizations have differences among them, the attribution of these differences to some form of *culture* is not supportable simply because other explanations can account for those same differences. In addition to that, organizations characterized as having different cultures have many institutional characteristics in common. For example, processes of accounting and production are carried out in fundamentally similar ways in all organizations.

The second problem with the concept of *culture* as applied to organizations is related to the unresolved argument over cultural determinism and the origins of cultural change. Old arguments in anthropology maintain that cultures cannot be changed on purpose and in prechosen directions (Harris, 1968). White (1948) argued that even though some people believe strongly that *culture* can be controlled, evidence for this conclusion is scarce if not nonexistent. Faith that advances in science, technology, and philosophy give people the power to shape their own destiny is a weakly supported belief in light of the two world wars and the Great Depression in the 20th century, and the ever-increasing and of unnecessary complexities in life such as fashion trends and entertainment media. All complex social entities can be traced back to earlier approximations. The United Nations can be traced back to tribal councils, modern warfare and weapons systems can be traced back to prehistoric people throwing rocks at each other, and complex national and international economic systems have grown out of all the barter and distribution processes used since before the Stone Age.

Culture, asserted White, cannot be explained in terms of humans. Humans have remained a constant element of *culture*. *Culture* cannot be explained in terms of environment. Environments have remained consistent while the cultures they have contained have changed dramatically. *Culture* must be explained in terms of *culture*; *culture* results from a social continuum. All cultural traits grow out of previous cultural traits or situations. *Culture* of the present was determined by *culture* of the past, and *culture* of the future will be determined by the past and the present. *Culture* makes itself. Although people cannot control the course of *culture*, they can learn to predict it, and even to make some adjustments. But understanding *culture* gives people no more control over it than understanding the ocean gives them control over the tides.

One of the better arguments in favor of cultural control was presented by Opler (1964). Opler argued that culture is not a deterministic entity that uniformly creates its members. People are not helpless, hapless recipients of *culture*. Rather, they are active shapers of the nature and boundaries of their social processes. "Culture is to be thought of less as a rigid cast than as a plastic border against which men strain" (p. 526). *Culture* is the work of humanity, it seems to be autonomous only because of our efforts to define and categorize it. However, straining against a plastic border is a much different proposition than managing that which the border contains. Opler implied that cultural outcomes are collectively determined by a sum total of movement within the culture and not rationally determined by a central controller.

While no evidence lends greater weight to either side of the argument, organizational studies maintain, as Schein did, the latter position for pragmatic reasons. If organizational culture cannot be changed on purpose, then what is there to offer managers who are seeking methods to improve performance? Whatever can be changed in an organization has been packaged as *organizational culture* for sale and distribution to managers. A manager can hire a high priced consultant who will claim to fix the organization's culture, but it does not follow that whatever is fixed is a *culture*.

The third problem is that, under any conditions, organizational culture can never be as comprehensive a source of behavior as social culture. Organization members have been extensively enculturated before walking through the door, and the organization can offer nothing within its boundaries except a modified take on external social roles and institutions. There is little in the way of role expectations inside the organization that cannot be understood or even anticipated by outsiders based on their knowledge of social culture.

Organizational socialization has been defined as a process where *outsiders* become *insiders* (Bullis & Stout, 2000). *Socialization,* if it were to happen in an organization, would necessarily replace (with the organization's version) metaphysical assumptions, foundational values, social institutions, and an essential *Weltanschauung* that the individual has been learning since childhood. Because this type of transformation rarely happens in organizations, a more appropriate word for the transition to membership status would be *initiation.*

Cultural anthropology, like analytical philosophy, is an artifact of Western culture. It began as an extension of the study of history, and is rooted in the philosophical developments of the Age of Enlightenment (Harris, 1968). Kroeber and Kluckhohn (1952) defined culture as a "set of attributes and products of human societies, and therewith of mankind, which are extrasomatic and transmissible by mechanisms other than biological heredity (p. 145). These authors maintained that such a concept was not to be found before the nineteenth century. However, Harris argued that what Kroeber and Kluckhohn proposed is not a concept as much as it is a theory of culture--that is, "an explanation of how the features of a particular population's behavioral repertory are fashioned, i.e., by learning rather than by genetic processes" (p. 10).

Schein (1986) defined organizational culture as "a pattern of basic assumptions--invented, discovered, or developed by a given group as it learns to cope with its problems of external adaptation and internal integration--that has worked well enough to be considered valid and, therefore, to be taught to new members as the correct way to perceive, think, and feel in relation to these problems" (p. 9). What Schein has proposed is a theory of *culture* as it is formulated in organizations without having made a case that one organizational culture can be distinguished from another except on the basis of teaching, learning, and problem solving.

If basic assumptions can be used to distinguish one *culture* from another, these assumptions are in place to address ontological problems and cannot be directly observed. They may only be known through the use of epistemological methods, which are necessarily specified by a particular *culture* as the conventional manner in which problems are solved. Cultural assumptions must be interpreted from the culture's artifacts, which include institutions of religion and institutions of knowledge. Given that virtually all American and European organizations use Baconian and Cartesian ontology and Newtonian methods to solve problems, one would be hard pressed to find *cultural* differences at the ontological level between Siemens and General Motors.

Methods of solving problems and acquiring knowledge tend to be consistent in a culture, and cultures can be distinguished by comparing their sources of knowledge and the applications of the knowledge they acquire. In the modern world, knowledge is acquired from one of two sources: knowledge is either revealed through experience or divine inspiration, or it is acquired using what may be called scientific method. Basic assumptions about the sources of knowledge are connected to other basic assumptions about the sources and operations of the cosmos. For an organization to employ a different cultural approach to solving problems, it would first need to establish a theology upon which to base its approach, and that theology would have to be embraced by all the organization's members.

All organizations in the Western world use some version of the scientific methods which have been handed down through Western philosophical traditions as a means to define problems, to identify and gather data, and to then solve the problems. The elements of this process were briefly discussed in Chapter One. Western organizations use scientific method because their members learned it in school as the correct way to solve problems. People who do not know the fundamentals of scientific methods and who believe that knowledge is acquired by consulting the stars, tarot cards, ancient writings, prophesies, or priests are generally not hired into Western organizations in any capacity where they would solve critical problems or be in a position to influence those who solve problems important to organizational outcomes, at least not officially. Although it can be argued that modern organizations have their versions of soothsayers in marketing and strategic planning, problem solving methods are artifacts brought into the organization from the social culture of its members.

Organizations may be distinguished according to their proficiency in using problem solving methods, but they cannot be said to be using different methods such that these methods represent different cultural approaches. If organizations invent, discover, or develop basic assumptions as Schein suggested, these assumptions certainly do not characterize ontological development as it is associated with *culture*. Rather, these assumptions account for structure as applied to problem solving on a level that presupposes answers to certain ontological and epistemological questions. A pattern of assumptions used for this kind of problem solving in an organization can be expected to vary over relatively short periods of time given changing business and industry conditions.

Schein proposed that culture is made up of essentially three things: artifacts, values, and assumptions. Most studies of organizational culture tend to focus almost exclusively on the artifacts--status meetings, coffee breaks, organizational structure, communication styles and networks, stories, symbols, rituals, language, etc. To imply that a thorough description of these artifacts is a description of the culture is like describing the ocean depths as having waves, whitecaps, and seagulls. Given that there is speculation on deepseated values, analyses generally do not go far enough in exploring the complexity of the social processes that produce those artifacts because the analysts are themselves limited by culturally derived values and methods.

For example, Kunda (1992) listed the elements of corporate *culture* training used in one organization: "What is a Techie. Getting Ahead. Networking. Being a Self-Starter. Taking Charge. How to Identify Burnout. The Subcultures. Presentations. Managing Your Career. Managing Your Boss. Women." (p. 6). This training module is accompanied by a *Culture Operating Manual*. The trainer was quoted: "My job is to marry them to the company" (p. 7). This approach is mistaking the processes of control and management of resources for that which defines what, out of all the things in the universe, constitutes a resource. This form of *cultural* training can in no way approximate the type of socialization that is formulated within a context of the cultural institutions of family, education, and religion.

Kunda suggested correctly that organizational culture is widely thought to be an issue of membership. *Membership* provides a more useful construct for organizational analysis. The concept of *membership* allows for anthropology to explain the influence of social institutions that invade rather than originate in organizations. There is no doubt that in modern times social culture and organizational behavior are linked in a reciprocal relationship. We see our fellow employees every day for most of our waking hours, but we do not *know* them in the same way that we *know* people of our own culture. If they belong to our culture, then we *know* them in that respect before they came to work in the organization. Restrictions imposed on behavioral choices by organizational structure and by the pursuit of goals not of our own choosing do not allow the sort of relationships or activities to develop among organization members that would be needed to create and to develop a *culture*.

It is structure that distinguishes organizations from merely groups of people who have common goals. In addition to defining organizational roles and the expectations which guide behavior, the structure provides conceptual boundaries that members can use to determine when they are *inside* the organization and when they are *outside* the organization. An organization member, Celia, knows she is *inside* the organization when she is working in her office; she is *outside* the organization when she is sitting at her desk speaking with her mother on the phone. When Celia travels to another organization to make a presentation, she is *inside* her organization. But, if she decides to visit a museum after the presentation, Celia is now *outside* the organization. Celia's behavior is determined to some degree by her perception of being *inside* or *outside* organizational boundaries.

In addition to being a member of an organization, Celia *belongs* to a culture (say, American). Having been socialized into the American culture from childhood, she is never *out* of it. When she travels to a pagoda in Japan or visits a cafe in Paris, she is still an American. Whether she is speaking with her boss in her office or with her children on a playground, she is still an American. *Socialization* results in permanent belonging. *Initiation* allows access--passage across the boundaries of the organization. Organizational membership is temporary. When Celia resigns or retires from her organization, she will never be *in* again even when she visits her old office. She will be an American until the day she dies.

Organizational differences can be assessed through a *characteristic pattern of decision making*. Patterns of decision making follow from consistently applied values and from action taken toward consistent objectives, therefore can be used to differentiate one organization from another. Patterns of communication may be distinctive among organizations. However, individuals from a given culture can also be distinguished on the basis of behavioral patterns. Using such organizational patterns allows for distinctions among organizations, but such a use does not necessarily support the concept of organizational culture.

Culture is something different. *Culture* is a medium through which artifacts and institutions are created, and through which resources, purposes, and thinking itself are defined. Anthropologists have great difficulties distinguishing *culture* from society and from personality because they are highly interrelated and because it is difficult to determine which causes which (Bidney, 1953; Bohannan, 1963). Bohannan used the analogy of electricity to characterize the problem. Electricity is difficult to define without referring to volts, ohms, and amperes. But a volt has no meaning without reference to ohms and amperes, and so on. The elements are so interrelated, that they cannot be understood independently.

Culture must not be confused with the outcomes of *culture* just as electricity must not be confused with the outcomes accomplished by electrical devices. It was through the medium of *culture* that ancient Greeks created and developed philosophy; it was through the medium of *culture* that philosophy was rejected in a principled way by Christian thinkers; it was through the medium of *culture* that philosophy was revived in the period of Enlightenment. All of those outcomes have been attributed to Western *culture*, yet the people involved in creating them operated on very different values and assumptions.

In this light, efforts to isolate and to define a leader's personality by empirical methods and to hold up the result as an example of *leadership* are entirely fruitless. It is the equivalent of choosing one volt of many and defining the characteristics of *that* volt without reference to ohms and amperes, and then holding up the result as an example of electricity. While *culture* constitutes the conditions and the context for leadership, it also constitutes the conditions and the context for *organization*. The question for the present chapter is, then, if organizations do not have cultures, what do they have?

The Organization As A Political Community

My original interest in explaining organizational behavior and outcomes was inspired by a question my boss asked me in 1982: "Why do these @#&* management effectiveness programs never work?" At various times I thought I had the answer, only to discover that the answer I had was unsatisfactory. The following development represents the latest amelioration in that succession of answers. It is a development of ideas generated as a result of reflection upon a longitudinal study of General Dynamics Corporation. Here, the treatment of the particulars of the study will be superficial, and the study itself should be taken as a vehicle toward an understanding with certain instructive findings. The focus of the case is less important than where it eventually leads.

There are at least two different issues to consider when developing ethics programs for organizations (Barker, 1993): rule following issues and quality of life issues. An evaluation of the Ethics Program at General

Dynamics concluded that the company was successful in meeting the program's specific objectives (i.e. bringing employees' behavior in line with a set of specific rules), but less than successful in meeting the program's implied goal of improving the quality of life for employees. The explanation of these results originally focused upon the contradictions built into the program--the goal-oriented, rational or rule-following intent of the program versus the expectations of employees for humanistic treatment and enhanced quality of life, and upon conflict between two "cultural" elements of the organization. A different explanation addresses the *point* of being in business vís-a-vís the *point* of doing work.

All organization members make decisions the collective manifestations of which fall into certain patterns that result in more or less consistent outcomes. The exploration of these patterns can be conducted using political frameworks. Deetz (1992) has asserted that organizations have, in many ways, replaced government. "Organizations make most decisions regarding the use of resources, the development of technologies, the products available, and the working relations among people" (p. 3). While it can be argued that a substantial portion of industrial technology is developed at the behest of the military, it is clear that organizations have taken on many roles heretofore expected of government. Deetz further suggested that the state's power is restricted to crude guidance through taxation and regulation. If that suggestion is accurate, then it may be instructive to think of the organization as something approaching a government.

What would Aristotle make of the modern organization? Clearly the structure of society he had in mind when he wrote *The Politics* (Aristotle, 1962) was something completely different than the structure of industrial society. However, it may be possible to speculate on how he might have applied his fundamental principles of governance to modern times.

Aristotle would certainly not regard a large and pluralistic country such as the USA or any industrial European country as the equivalent of a city/state (hereafter referred to as a *polis*--a political community). A *polis*, he said, "must have a population large enough to cater for all the needs of a self-sufficient existence, but not so large that it cannot be easily supervised" (VII,4). It is doubtful even that he would regard the USA as culturally homogeneous enough to provide support to a *polis* similar to that provided to Athens by Hellenic culture. He might, however, consider an organization to be a form of *polis*.

To begin with, Aristotle advocated slavery as an important economic tool for support of the *polis*. While we in industrial society believe that owning people is immoral, we have no moral problem with the concept of the organization "owning" an employee for a specified period of time each day. Substituting the words *supervisor* for master and *subordinate* for slave, the characteristics of this intermittent ownership are scarcely discernable from Aristotle's slavery: The master/slave relationship is a reciprocal relationship united by a common interest (they cannot do without each other); above all subordinates must be obedient-- not being obedient is grounds for termination; subordinates must perform only tasks specified by their supervisors and not other tasks; subordinates may not slack from performing these tasks; subordinates must perform these tasks when ordered to perform them and within the time period allotted; and, except under certain conditions, subordinates may not supplement their work with activities of their own choosing.

Many employers feel justified imposing restrictions on personal relationships among their subordinates, and on their affiliations with other organizations. We will go as far as to collectively agree that employees are stealing from employers (acting immorally) when they are involved in unauthorized activities such as shopping on the internet, conversing on the phone with friends, or simply staring out the window daydreaming. It should also be noted that Aristotle's slave had certain legal rights, and could bring litigation against the master under the appropriate circumstances. In some cases, the slaves won their suits.

The differences between the Athenian and the industrial forms of slavery are, in theory, first a mutually agreed upon compensation to the industrial subordinate for the specific conditions of the relationship, and second an abstract idea, known as the *employment at will* doctrine, that allows the industrial relationship to be perceived as voluntary. Surveys of employees, however, usually indicate that they feel underpaid for their work. Further, there are but three alternatives to subordination in an organization: first, to be a subordinate in another organization, second, to become the master by starting your own organization, or third, to be homeless.

Slavery was not only important economically for Aristotle, but it represented the natural order of things. "He that can by his intelligence foresee things needed is by nature a ruler and master, while he whose bodily strength enables him to perform them is by nature a slave" (I,2). The organizational chart is a sophisticated method for establishing, conventionalizing, and validating the master/slave relationship. Thus, the

.

natural order of things can be graphically represented with the *leader* at the top.

Because Aristotle considered business to be a "household" activity and not a political activity, it is tempting to consider the organization as a representation of Aristotle's household, which is the repository of slavery. But then we are left with having to make political communities out of pluralistic entities that Aristotle would not abide, or have no *polis* at all. There is no close fit on either side, but there are important indicators.

We can begin by agreeing with Aristotle that the *polis* is a natural outcome of the natural human desire for political association (as a potential vehicle for *eudaimonia*). Proceeding on this tact implies that organizations are much more than simply economic entities, and views of the organizational role in society must include more than that role conceptualized by Friedman (1970) and others. Organizations provide not only an opportunity for people to subsist, but opportunities for them to experience growth. A person with no *polis* is, after Homer, without family, without morals, and without home. People we call *homeless* are not necessarily without shelter and other resources, more specifically they are not members of any organization.

Aristotle defined the *polis* in a number of similar ways, but we can accept that it is "a community of some kind, and every community is established with a view to some good" (I,1). The purpose, or *point*, of the *polis* is of supreme importance in distinguishing it from other social entities; "the state or political community, which is the highest of all, and which embraces all the rest, aims, and in a greater degree than any other, at the highest good" (I,1). The purpose, or *point*, of an organization is, or should be, much more than simply serving customers and making profits (Deming, 1986).

The organization is defined by its constitution, and it has a number of specific characteristics. For one, it is of a manageable size, as eluded to above. For another, it limits the membership of citizens. "We do not for a moment accept the notion that we must give the name citizen to all persons whose presence is necessary for the existence of the state" (III,5). States have little in common, so in each case the citizen is defined by the constitution. Aristotle would limit citizenship in a number of ways, but he defined a citizen as "one who has the ability and the chance to participate in government" (III,5). In a truly democratic organization (which Aristotle would not recommend) that might include all employees. In an ideal organization, Aristotle would limit citizenship to managers and certain professionals--what he would call an aristocracy.

Aristotle was not an avid fan of moneymaking. The wealth sought by capitalists he would consider a tool with limits to its use. Wealth should be used for administration of the state, aimed at pursuing a supreme good. Because the state exists for the sake of the common good, wealth can facilitate noble deeds. The state cannot be a naturally subject or servile institution, but must be self-directed and independent. Therefore, Aristotle might agree that economic wealth, and subsequent power, helps establish some form of independence and self-determination for organizations in a complex, pluralistic society.

Organizational Constitutions

To Aristotle, the *polis* is defined by its constitution, which organizes those living in the *polis*. "Constitution is the arrangement which states adopt for the distribution of offices of power, and for the determination of sovereignty and of the end which the whole social complex in each case aims at realizing" (IV,1). There are basically three types of constitutions: (1) monarchy, ruled by one person, (2) aristocracy, ruled by a small but elite group, and (3) democracies, ruled by some majority of people. Aristotle favored the aristocracy because he felt it was the most effective form for solving problems, and because it most closely represents the natural order of things. There are three elements to constitutions: (1) deliberative, the policy making process, (2) executive, the bureaucracy of administrative officials who carry out policy, and (3) judicial, the enforcement of policy and the distribution of justice.

The *constitution* of an organization is defined by its charter and by its strategic and operating plans, the sum of which include its mission, its standard operating policies and procedures, its organizational chart (structure), and its personnel manual. The charter and plans cover the deliberative, executive, and judicial elements of the constitution. Deming (1986) would suggest that the constitution of an organization provides for its "constancy of purpose"--the *point* of being in business in the first place.

There are basically three types of organizations: (1) monarchies, run by entrepreneurs or autocrats, (2) aristocracies, run chiefly by some combination of boards of directors, executives, and organizational managers (this type has many varieties), and (3) democracies, run by some constitutional form of employee consensus. Determination of a specific organization's type for the purposes of measurement should be guided by some assessment of attitudes toward the supervisor/subordinate relationship from both sides of that relationship. There were many beloved masters in the history of slavery. True democracies will have few, if any, symbols used to determine and to enforce differences in status, and will have institutionalized methods of achieving consensus.

Neither Aristotle nor Plato favored democracies because they considered a large portion of the population not up to the task of governing. Just as Athenian democracy excluded women and slaves from governance, so modern organizations generally exclude wage earners and low level professionals from the governance and decision making processes. In both cases, lower levels of the hierarchy are not trusted to be capable of making correct judgements and decisions. This ancient idea reinforces modern notions that *leaders* are the ones upon whom we should rely for decision making.

Sharing common views of good and bad, right and wrong, just and unjust is what makes a *polis*. "Right is the basis of political association and right is the criterion for deciding what is just" (I,2). Justice in some conventional form is essential for the state. In an organization, justice manifests itself in compensation, assignment of tasks and responsibilities, selection, promotion, termination, quality, civic responsibility, and customer relations.

Aristotle was opposed to homogeneity as a goal for the *polis*: "You cannot make a state out of men who are all alike" (II,2). Plurality is natural for the state, and a high degree of moral conformity would remove that which is vital and which promotes growth. "It is a perfect balance between its different parts that keeps a state in being" (II,2).

Two essentials for the state (VII,4) are a supply of labor, and a territory. The workforce supplies the labor for an organization, and the territory is defined by organizational boundaries, assets, and market share. Additional essential parts (VII,8) include the following:

(a) Food--the sustenance. Food is the primary output of the state; it is needed to keep both citizen and slave healthy and able to work on the state's behalf. In the case of organizations, we can cite raw materials and supplies that are converted to products as that which is needed to sustain the striving for goals.

(b) Tools and crafts--the technology used to make products.

(c) Arms--for protection and acquisition of new territory. Protection of the organization is provided by marketing and legal departments. The legal department is designed to protect the organization's assets from invasion and capture, and the marketing department is designed to protect existing market share and to acquire more if possible. Other arms include insurance, lobbying, public relations, and advertising.

(d) Wealth--capital. Wealth is a tool used to accomplish the objectives of the state.

(e) Religion--that which guides normal behavior and explains the unexplainable. Religion in an organization is not quite the comprehensive institution that it normally represents for a society. The organization's religion amounts to an official dogma that encapsulates the organization's construction of reality. Elaborate belief systems regarding organizational purposes and outcomes are constructed to which citizens adhere. As with any religion, these beliefs need not be supported by empirical evidence. An organization that routinely cheats customers and stockholders can portray itself as socially responsible. Citizens practice this religion by reciting doctrinal rhetoric whenever possible, and especially on religious occasions such as monthly reviews and shareholder meetings. An example of this would be tobacco company executives testifying before Congress that they did not believe that smoking causes disease. Failing to adhere to dogmatic teachings or to perform ceremonial utterances can bring charges of heresy, impiety, and not being a team player. One of the ways a citizen can be distinguished from a slave is by the degree of adherence to the organization's religion.

(f) Justice--a method of arriving at decisions about policy and about right and wrong. This element is the most important of this list because in it are manifested the essential values and assumptions used in decision making. Justice is defined by the constitution, and from its definition flows all essential outcomes of the organization.

Organizational Citizens

Aristotle devoted a good deal of thought to the nature of the citizen and to the system of education needed for developing the best citizens. Aristotle defined citizens as those who participate in the management of the *polis*. Participation is not merely an obligation--as in showing up for work--but takes the form of habitually virtuous behavior. That is, citizenship is defined more by what a person does than by what a person is. The question of conduct centers about the contribution (or the perception of contribution) a person makes to the overall goals of the organization. Those citizens who contribute most are entitled to a larger share of the wealth than those who contribute less, or than those who are not citizens. Therefore, justice is governed according to virtuous participation, and distribution of wealth and power is based in some concept of merit.

Those whom we identify as citizens will be different from each other, and will necessarily have differing levels of skills and abilities. Citizens must be educated and prepared through institutionalized means maintained by the *polis*, and education must be comprehensive; a citizen must learn not only to rule, but to be ruled (III,4). All those entitled to be citizens must be able, willing, and prepared to assimilate the roles and duties specified under the constitution. While each citizen has a different function, there is a common definition applicable to all within the context of the *polis*. So, the virtue of the citizen must be judged relative to the *polis* of which she or he is a member. Since each *polis* is different, according to Aristotle, there cannot be one simple perfect virtue of all good citizens. Citizenship, as with virtue, is a relative issue.

Compiling An Idea

What do we have so far? Ethics are sources of identity and motivation for mature individuals, representing some sense of prevailing *telos*. A person develops an ethic by learning cultural convention and then modifies what has been learned according to insight and personal experience. The *point* is often taken for granted; a good deal of that which influences the development of an ethic is not likely to be grasped consciously by the individual. For individuals, ethics establish states of existence that make them, for example, more or less predisposed to accept or reject authority and supervision of their activities. Ethics guide individuals toward that which is likely to provide them with *eudaimonia*, and away from that which will not. Ethics induce people to seek out the association of others who share similar ethics.

Morals are codes of conduct that encourage and protect choices of association. People learn morals by consciously assimilating conventional standards, by constructing their habitual behavior around these standards, and by adapting behavior according to their understanding of those standards. People learn to sort out behavioral standards relative to social role expectations and social contexts that exist within a given *telos*. Moral systems result from repetitive, customary behavior that becomes institutionalized through political associations. Structured moral institutions are embodied in the constitution of the *polis* to perpetuate the moral order, and to provide for the welfare of the citizens of the *polis*.

These institutions are not necessarily developed through conscious planning and intervention, they can very well be outcomes that were intended specifically by no one.

Organizations, to varying degrees, represent political associations and opportunities for political activity that cannot otherwise be experienced or constructed by individuals within the greater society. While conventional knowledge holds that organizations are narrowly purposeful and rationally managed entities, research reveals processes that can best be explained as political activity (Barker, 1993 & 1994; Jackall, 1988):

(a) Functional groups compete for ascendancy of ideas, influence, and resources, which is characterized by conflict.

(b) The level of power and influence of any one manager depends upon that individual prevailing in conflicts regularly.

(c) The corporate and bureaucratic structures are set up by and for those with the most controlling power.

(d) Success or failure of managers has little to do with actual accomplishments, but rather with arbitrary perceptions of one's ability by others and with supportive alliances (that is, success and failure are socially defined, not empirically measured).

(e) Truth is socially constructed and the organization mobilizes to support a manufactured reality promoted by those in power.

(f) Uncertainty in the organization and in management processes facilitates redefinition of organizational reality.

(g) Therefore, decisions are based in political agreement, and agreement is based in comparative power and influence.

Jackall found that the moral system for managers in bureaucratic organizations includes some of the following principles:

(a) Striving for success is a moral imperative.

(b) Rising stars serve to validate the moral system.

(c) Criteria for success are bounded by the system and can be based in illusion rather than in reality--success is often the result of taking credit for the good and avoiding blame for the bad.

(d) Self-control, and not necessarily rule following behavior, is a moral imperative.

(e) Morality is measured by flexibility and adaptability to changing political realities, and not by strong convictions.

(f) Bad things must be covered up or reframed in order to protect the system.

(g) Morality is a matter of survival and gaining advantage.

For the citizen of this *polis*, morality has different implications than it does for those we may call *employees*, which Aristotle might recognize as slaves. While all employees may be initiated as organizational members, only a select few will undergo extensive initiation to achieve the status of *citizen*.

In the General Dynamics study, employees at lower levels of the organization expected their quality of life to improve as a result of the Ethics Program (Barker, 1993). The failure of their expectations to be realized was commonly attributed by them to immoral behavior on the part of managers. These employees had not been indoctrinated into citizenship. Most never would be. Consequently, they understood the basic customs which govern the masses, but not the constitutional protocol the political elite are expected to observe and follow.

Middle and senior level managers at General Dynamics, who were citizens, commonly viewed the Ethics Program as simply another political obligation. Instead of an opportunity for improvement, most managers experienced the program as yet another uncertainty to be managed in their quest to succeed. Their conformance to the rules established by the program was established by the constitution, and their experience of justice was directly related to which of their behaviors were measured and rewarded by the *polis*.

Supervisors were citizens-in-training, and were caught between their understanding of the desires of employees for improved quality of life and their realization that the political goal of the program was to improve customer relations with the Navy in particular and with the Pentagon in general--that is, to improve the quality of life for citizens and not necessarily for the masses. The decisions of the *polis* were governed by the need to survive and to protect its territory. The welfare of the masses was secondary to this goal, and was considered ultimately irrelevant should the *polis* fail.

Connecting The Vessel With The Engine

A tempting conclusion about organizational behavior and about business ethics is that people tend to feel morally justified doing anything necessary to survive in a state of self-interested competition no matter what harm it may cause others. This conclusion is consistent with observations of managerial behavior that is either unregulated or only partially regulated (e.g. Jackall, 1988; Kaufman, 1973). Given this conclusion, it is inherent upon some regulatory agency to establish rules and laws. The perceived role of government as a regulatory agency encourages the legal approach to business ethics, which tends to predominate the view of many authors (Donaldson, 1982). The legal approach is the next best thing to natural law for those opposed to relativity in moral theory. But the legal approach does not account for variation in laws or for contradictory regulations, nor does it distinguish between those who test the legal limits and those who are truly virtuous. It is one thing to believe that God has imposed universal law, it is quite another to imply that a government or an organization has done the same thing.

Organizations are often perceived as moral entities with responsibilities that transcend laws, something one would expect from a *polis* with an intact constitution. If the organization is indeed a political community, then morality must be expected to occur within the sphere of relativity applied to any sovereign nation that shares some connection with other nations from whom those expectations are warranted. Moral behavior in organizations results from a complex interplay between that which facilitates employee support and actions (membership) and that which specifies rules, systems, and standard operating procedures designed primarily to regulate behavior, to minimize uncertainty, and to support existing power structures (constitution). When behavior is perceived to be based in self-interest by outsiders, it is often perceived as loyalty to organizational objectives by insiders (Jackall, 1988). Conditions of citizenship demand assimilation of organizationally constructed reality as applied to goals, and of constitutional justice as applied to the behavior expected in the achievement of those goals.

Industrial society has reframed ethics from an issue of happiness to an issue of property. Organizations are political communities which facilitate the creation and acquisition of property, and its translation into identity. Property must be defined broadly here as any tangible asset used toward the accomplishment of goals; the goals may be getting ahead, making money, or noble deeds. Property can be distinguished from *eudaimonia* in that the latter is a sensation that does not have a specific object. That people acquire property and still do not experience *eudaimonia* reinforces the idea that they are different things, and that the former is the conventional measure of achievement.

The *constitution* conveys conventional knowledge about moral behavior, and about how social and management problems are to be addressed within organizational boundaries. The *constitution* is both the result and the author of collective action within organizational boundaries.

The *constitution* provides the essential components of structure and of decision making, and specifies how those influence behavior. Moral assessment of organizational behavior must take into consideration requirements for citizenship that are built into the moral system apart from the rules and regulations. Morality cannot be assessed apart from consideration of the motivation to behave.

To answer my boss's original question--why do management effectiveness programs never work?: Managers who create the programs, the language and symbols used to sell and to represent the programs to others, and the method of implementation usually have no intention of changing the fundamental *constitution* of the organization, which provides the structure for their authority, the conditions for their continued status as citizens, the rational for their behavior, and the *point* of being in business.

Organizational analysis must center on defining the *constitution*, which provides the essential components of structure, of decision making, and of those influences on behavior over and above the *culture* to which organization members belong before they come to the organization. Assessment of organizational behavior must take into consideration requirements for citizenship that are built into the organization's systems apart from specific rules and regulations. Organizations should be redefined as centers of political life that provide average people with opportunities for *eudaimonia*.

Chapter 4

Convention In The Study and Practice of Leadership

Conventional knowledge is the common rationality as applied to human actions within a cultural milieu (Giddens, 1987). As with all other constructs, the understanding of leadership as it is applied to industrial society depends upon conventional *theories* to support its internal integrity, and to establish its truth. Mainstream leadership study is designed to establish the conventional knowledge needed by actors in this specific social system. Leadership scholars discuss Leadership Quotient, or Transformational Leadership, or Leader-Member Exchange theory, and practioners adopt the roles specified within these models as the correct approach to the study and practice of leadership.

At some point in the past, when humans wandered the earth in search of subsistence, our needs were literally *our* needs. We required no explanation of what we needed or how to act; our needs and the actions required to fulfill those needs demanded no justification. When agrarian societies began to apply superstition to an understanding of the natural processes that affected the harvest, our attention shifted from *our* needs to the needs of the gods. The notion that something powerful out there is creating outcomes was combined with the idea that powerful people we know can create outcomes. Our *leader*, then, was the person who explained to us how we must act in order to satisfy the gods so that they might favor us with abundance. As society developed a feudal structure, the roles of *leader* and *god* merged. The needs of the king became synonymous with (or perhaps took precedence over) the needs of the gods. Samuel warned of this shift when the Jews asked that the God of Abraham provide them with a flesh and blood king.

If you insist on having a king, he will conscript your sons and make them run before his chariots; some will be made to lead his troops into battle, while others will be slave laborers; they will be forced to plow in the royal fields, and harvest his crops without pay; and make his weapons and chariot equipment. He will take your daughters from you and force them to cook and bake and make perfumes for him. He will take away the best of your fields and vineyards and olive groves and give them to his friends. He will take a tenth of your harvest and distribute it to his favorites. He will demand your slaves and the finest of your youth and will use your animals for his personal gain. He will demand a tenth of your flocks, and you shall be his slaves. You will shed bitter tears because of this king you are demanding, but the Lord will not help you" (1 Samuel 8:11).

Even so, the people wanted a king to govern them and to lead them into battle, and Samuel's warning anticipated that which would be eventually called *leadership*. The king's core needs were fairly simple: to acquire and to control land and its subsequent economic wealth. In feudal Europe, the king's needs were justified to us by the institution of the church, which by that time had become much more than simply a religion devised to explain God's needs.

In the industrial era, the needs we are expected to fulfill are defined for us by our economic institutions. In modern times, one is required to endure twelve or more years of school to learn how to meet institutional needs. The role of the church as interpreter has diminished, and the role of the king is commonly shifted to CEOs. Needs are now defined as a function of technology and as a function of a consumer based economy. Our needs as human beings are subordinated to the needs of corporations and other institutions, and this subordination is justified to us by the various agents and interpreters of our institutions (which ultimately include any form of government guided by economic ideology). We have accepted this shift in the hierarchy of needs, just as the Jews accepted their new king, and we have adapted to its demands. Leaders are promoted as agents of institutional needs, and *ethical leaders* are admonished to adjust organizational needs to meet human needs as much as possible. However, few managers who expect to keep their positions will place subordinate's needs over organizational needs.

Conventional understanding of leadership has been systematically constructed from other conventional knowledge about social hierarchies and about their command and control structures. This knowledge has then been used to validate leadership theories without further critical analysis.

The development of leadership *truth* has been a cyclical process of using convention that has been the source of development also as the source of validation.

Conventional leadership scholars most consistently agree upon one thing: leaders are supposed to *motivate* followers/subordinates to accomplish organizational goals. House and Aditya (1997) summarized the history of leadership study, discussing different approaches to assessing the leader's ability to motivate subordinates, but without addressing specific sources of motivation. Most theories of motivation attribute that which energizes and sustains behavior to internally experienced needs. Many leadership theories cited by House and Aditya hold that it is the leader's job to orient and/or to satisfy those needs in such a way as to extract the desired goal-oriented behavior from subordinates.

House and Aditya did not address the possibility that the leader might do such a good job satisfying subordinate needs, that motivation to work toward objectives would dissipate, or would at least be directed elsewhere. Socrates addressed this possibility by defining love as "desire for the perpetual possession of the good" (Plato, 1951, p. 86). Love, in the sense meant by Socrates, is what motivates a person to take an action toward an object or end. The key to this definition is the implication that if desire is ever satisfied--if one actually did perpetually possess the good--what remains is not love or, more specifically, not motivation.

Modern management activity must not completely satisfy needs, or its own purpose would be defeated. House and Aditya also did not speculate on the degree of satisfaction needed to maintain contentment while leaving enough experience of need to continue to stimulate motivation. Assumptions that leaders can manipulate subordinate motivation and the recommendations for accomplishing that manipulation probably oversimplify the whole issue of motivational forces. But, these sorts of assumptions are exemplary of conventional ideas that place the leader in control of outcomes. When research is conducted on the issue, the simple assertion that the leader is responsible for achieving goals is used to verify the leader's involvement in motivation, thus reinforcing the whole concept.

House and Aditya did not attempt to establish a definition of leadership, but concluded with the following statement: "A problem with current leadership study is that it continues to focus excessively on superior-subordinate relationships to the exclusion of several functions that leaders perform and to the exclusion of organizational and environmental variables that are crucial to effective leadership performance" (p. 460). While these authors are attempting to stimulate new approaches to leadership study, in this rather typical statement they reinforce the key elements of conventional leadership wisdom: (a) that leadership is all about the leaders and their *functions* in the organization, (b) that the leader's performance is the sum total of leadership, and (c) that performance is the result of some characteristics of the leader vís-a-vís conditions of the environment. These elements might apply more readily to Aristotle's citizen, except that the industrial leader's goals are usually economic in character.

The aim of industrial leadership is to serve institutional needs. Pursuant to this aim, knowledge of institutions has been one source for the development of leadership theory. Unlike critical philosophy, critical history, or critical science, leadership theories have not generally been examined for anything other than the extent of their contribution toward their aim. Industrial leadership research, as described by Bass (1990), is primarily an exercise in *experimenta lucifera*, or light shedding experiments, that is obsessed with fact finding and conducted in such a way that competing theories are not examined. In this way, industrial leadership is a conventional paradigm, but not a science.

The pursuit of institutional needs proceeds under the presumption that the satisfied institution ultimately will meet individual wants and needs. However, institutions are designed to meet an *average* of individual needs, and not a specific individual's needs. Conventional experience of leadership is thought to be consistent with the degree to which a given individual experiences the satisfaction of needs. But the study of leadership tends to overlook the affect of the potential dichotomy between individual needs and institutional needs. In fact, the dichotomy itself is seen as a *leadership challenge*. One goal for industrial leaders is to persuade subordinates to replace their desire to pursue their individual needs with the desire to pursue institutional needs. Further, institutional *leaders* have slowly but surely facilitated a deterioration of an individual's ability to meet his or her own needs independent of institutions, part of the learned helplessness discussed by Gemmill and Oakley.

Given that many leadership scholars do not define leadership (Rost, 1991), they must necessarily be relying upon conventional knowledge to assess the validity of *leadership* activities. Those who act out *leadership* need not fully understand the minutia of this convention to be in a position to contribute to its validation. Leadership research in its traditional form is ultimately a ponderous confirmation of the conventional paradigm and little else. Whether leadership study is intended to be a marketing tool or is simply the hapless result of unscrutinized conventional dogma and misguided research methodology, its future is changing.

Conventional Knowledge About Leadership

The conventional view holds that leadership is an ability, specifically an ability to supervise the activities of others. Authors who do not define leadership usually take this notion to be self-evident, and therefore do not feel compelled to clarify any further. Even though the words *process* and *relationship* appear in many definitions, industrial leadership is assumed to be an ability of the leader to do something or to bring something about. In fact, industrial theories of leadership are more accurately labeled as theories of supervision. The following discussion is intended not only to illustrate the development of conventional knowledge about leadership, but to heighten the reader's awareness of the ways in which language is used to support convention and to suggest variety that does not really exist. The process of leadership will specifically be discussed in Chapter Five, and the leadership relationship will be discussed in Chapter Six.

In his *Handbook of Leadership*, Bass (1990) organized the work on leadership study into eight sections. The first section includes various concepts, definitions, and theories of leadership. Each concept is presented, some are related to each other, but none is developed to indicate a conceptual framework or theme for the remainder of the book. There is no discussion of ontological foundations for leadership study or any attempt to establish a firm epistemological position for conducting research. There is certainly no effort to clarify a definition. The first section gives a brief look at famous people in history, behavior of animals (pecking order and such), and sets the tone for the remainder of the book by insisting that "leaders do make a difference" (p. 8).

The second section is devoted to personal attributes of leaders. The third considers power and legitimacy, but the consideration emphasizes the leader's skill or ability to manage power and conflict rather than presenting power and conflict as contextual issues with interactive influence on outcomes. The fourth is about transactional exchange, where leadership is understood as the result of exchanges of valued things and leaders are defined by their ability to bargain. The fifth is about leadership and management style, and centers upon the personal values and activities of the person in charge. The sixth discusses situational moderators, but these moderators are viewed as things that either enhance or inhibit elements of a leader's style and not as a general context within which leadership or other social processes develop. The seventh is about diverse groups, but it is more about individual (cultural or personality) differences in leadership style than about what leadership might mean in different cultures. The final section is about leadership study in the future and will be discussed later.

Bass legitimized and defended conventional knowledge about the industrial paradigm of leadership. The industrial paradigm of leadership is based in an obsession with the persona of kings and conquerors that can be traced at least as far back as Biblical times. Until the Age of Enlightenment, people thought that "the anointed one" in charge was actually ordained by God as described in the Books of Samuel. For Thomas Aquinas (1952), unquestioning obedience to those in authority was a moral obligation because power is given to them by God. If this is a bad leader, then it is God's responsibility to take care of the problem, not subordinates'. This is the Christian notion of the hierarchy and command structure of the universe.

In the early 16th Century, Machiavelli (1981) was condemned by the church primarily because he removed leadership from the realm of God and placed it within the sphere of human activities, thereby setting the stage for industrial theories of leadership. He had carefully examined the behavior of princes and circumstances surrounding successful and unsuccessful principalities to create a theory of leadership. Machiavelli's audacity was to suggest that common people could become princes by virtue of their abilities and through the skillful application of specific principles: the successful leader "must have no other object or thought, nor acquire skill in anything, except war, its organization, and its discipline. The art of war is all that is expected of a ruler; and it is so useful that besides enabling hereditary princes to maintain their rule it frequently enables ordinary citizens to become rulers" (p. 87).

Machiavelli based his observations on several conventional assumptions, many of which can be traced back to Aristotle, that remain fairly well intact today:

(1) The leader's primary goal is to maintain and to expand the territory of the kingdom. In the industrial world, the kingdom is the organization, and its territory consists of market share and financial and material assets.

(2) The leader sits atop a hierarchy that is naturally ordered according to principles of Heaven. The leader has this position by virtue of ability. In the industrial world, the leader is ostensively defined as "the person at the top," whether it is the top of a small department or the top of a large corporation.

(3) The well-being of society is directly connected to each member's relationship with his or her leader. Assumed *natural* differences in knowledge and ability demand obedience and subordination to the higher authority for the coordinated protection of the kingdom.

(4) The leader must be free to choose any course of action she or he considers to be the best approach to solving the problems of the kingdom. This freedom is maintained through social detachment and through disconnection from any obligation to consider potential impact upon the subordinates. Leaders are contemptible if they appear to be weak, indecisive, fickle, trifling, or too emotionally attached to their subjects.

(5) Since the only real moral obligation for a leader is to maintain the kingdom, the morality of the leader's actions is only considered relative to the broad goals of the kingdom's survival and flourishing. Usually the leader's goals are necessarily the kingdom's goals.

In contrast to *The Prince*, Machiavelli revealed a different side of his thinking in *The Discourses* (Machiavelli, 1950). Machiavelli stressed virtues of the monarchy in *The Prince* primarily to impress Lorenzo Di Medici for the purpose of gaining favorable treatment and possibly employment, which is to say that he wrote what he thought the Prince wanted to hear. Otherwise, he supported a democratic republic. Main points he made in *The Discourses* include the following:

(1) The democratic republic is superior to every other form of government.

(2) All monarchies and authoritarian regimes still must rely upon the consent of the governed.

(3) Cohesiveness and unified purposefulness are primary imperatives for maintaining stability and for ensuring the survival of the state.

(4) The health and well being of the state depends upon the skills of the law-giver.

(5) A good citizen is one who will set aside personal feelings and act for the good of the state.

(6) To survive, the state depends on its vigilance and readiness for war.

(7) The purpose of religion for the state is to motivate the masses--religion is less important theologically than it is as a force that unifies the masses and supports their morale.

(8) Even in a democracy, ruthless measures may be needed to ensure survival.

(9) The state rises, becomes successful, becomes corrupt, falls, and is rejuvenated continuously as a natural cycle.

Given the industrial view of leadership, it should not be surprising that *The Prince* has been one of the most widely discussed books in the Western world (even though many of those who discuss it in modern times have not read it). *The Prince* describes the techniques used to run feudal and industrial organizations. *The Discourses* remains virtually unknown to the average college graduate. Certainly the latter work is consistent with many modern democratic ideals, but the former provides specific observations and premises that support conventional knowledge about what a leader is and what a leader does relative to power politics. Rhetoric regarding the inappropriateness of the approaches outlined in *The Prince* seems to be largely a smoke screen intended to distract attention from what amounts to a manual of trade secrets used by feudal and industrial leaders to accomplish their ends. If the content of *The Prince* were untrue or unusable, the text would have faded from modern view just as hundreds of its contemporaries have, including *The Discourses*.

Since the time of Machiavelli, leadership theorists have incorporated dimensions of context and of *followers*, but for the most part they have sought an explanation of leadership as the relationship between the persona (abilities, traits, characteristics, and actions) of the "man in charge," and the outcomes of the social milieu within which "he" appears to operate (his governance). This presumed cause-effect relationship is the source of conventional knowledge about leadership. On the one hand, trait theories are often criticized as inadequate means for understanding leadership (Bass, 1981; Bennis, 1959; Mintzberg, 1982; Rost, 1991; Stogdill, 1948), while on the other hand leadership scholars are flailing away at mounds of traits. In one survey of the literature, Fleishman, Mumford, Zaccaro, Levin, Korotkin, and Hein (1991) listed 499 traits or dimensions of leader behavior from 65 different systems.

Kotter (1988), defined leadership as "the process of moving a group (or groups) of people in some direction through (mostly) noncoercive means" (p. 16). Kotter acknowledged that the word *leadership* sometimes refers to people who occupy the roles where leadership by the first definition is expected. Kotter then characterized *good* or *effective* leadership as a process that "moves people in a direction that is genuinely in their real long-term best interests" (p. 17). As an example of effective leadership, Kotter chose Lee Iacocca. His rationale for this choice was Iacocca's apparent role in "an extraordinarily dramatic and very impressive turnaround" (p. 17).

Despite Kotter's use of the word *process* in his definition, he was clearly relying upon the characteristics of a great man doing great things to verify his construct. In addition, if effective leadership moves people toward their own best interests, then we are left to assume that the *processes* at Chrysler during the Iacocca era mobilized organizational activities and resources toward pursuit of the best interests of all of its employees. If leadership is fundamentally noncoercive, then we can be assured that these employees cheerfully carried out their organizational assignments with vivid images, perhaps even direct experience, of their common good. I, personally, would not expect to find Scott Adams' comic strip on the walls in any cubicle in such an organization.

The argument against questioning such applications of conventional knowledge is similar to that used in other institutionalized disciplines: any theoretical development that does not pay homage to the narrative or empirical traditions in the field is not valid. One hundred years of leadership theory development based upon the assumption that leadership is necessarily a function of the persona of the leader cannot be summarily dismissed, the argument goes, because this development has been the result of sincere and thoughtful effort by brilliant and capable scholars.

But the most sincere and thoughtful scholarship can be dismissed if its foundation assumptions are contradictory, poorly supported, or simply wrong. For example, several hundred years worth of sincere scholarship was founded on the assumption that the earth was the center of the universe. Just as geocentric theory was based in the understandable but incorrect perception of the sun and stars circling the earth, leadership theory has been based in the understandable but incorrect perception of a direct cause/effect relationship between the leader's abilities, traits, and actions and leadership outcomes.

When leadership is defined, the definition usually addresses the nature of the *leader* and the leader's abilities, and not the nature of *leadership*. For example, Wills (1994), after a lengthy discussion of what *leadership* is about, why *leadership* is important, and what *leadership* concerns, boldly declared "it is time for a definition: the leader is one who mobilizes others toward a goal shared by leaders and followers" (p.17). This definition of the leader, incidently, was not developed further, but taken to be self-evident.

The assumption that the leader is the source of leadership also implies that the leader is defined by position in a hierarchy and/or authority in a social system: "There he discovers that Leo, whom he had known first as *servant*, was in fact the titular head of the Order, its guiding spirit, a great and noble *leader*" (Greenleaf, 1995, p. 19). This statement about the plot of Hermann Hesse's *Journey to the East* was used by Greenleaf to illustrate how he concluded that leaders are servants first. This idea is very consistent with Aristotle's insistence that citizens learn to be commanded as well as to command. Greenleaf suggested that Leo was a great leader because of a particular trait; he was "by nature a servant" (p. 19). But even when he was the servant, "Leo was actually the leader all of the time" (p. 19). While leaders may practice humility, they are still presumed to be in charge. Leo was portrayed as much more than simply a citizen of a *polis*. Attempts to refute the assumption of hierarchy only serve to confuse the issue: "Leadership is, as you know, not a position but a job" (DePree, 1992, p. 7).

While some time ago traits were thought to be insufficient to explain leadership (Stogdill, 1948), traits have made a comeback as a primary explanation of leadership (Gemmill & Oakley, 1992; Kirkpatrick & Locke, 1991). Gemmill and Oakley likened the fascination with traits to a *ghost dance* intended to restore and to prevent disintegration of a civilization that is slipping away--one that celebrates the notion of superhuman heros who have the power to save us and to restore the past that will bring us comfort. Alarm about a "lack of leadership" is a sign of increasing social despair and massive learned helplessness.

Kirkpatrick and Locke (1991) identified six traits they believed differentiate leaders from other people: drive, motivation, honesty and integrity, self-confidence, cognitive ability, and knowledge of business. The assumption behind this form of research is that people will change their personalities and world views to adopt these traits and to become successful leaders (Rost, 1993). But, as Rost pointed out, the traits and abilities that presumably identify an effective leader cannot be substantially differentiated from those that define an effective manager, or an effective person.

How can we be sure these are the right traits? Do people who do not have these traits become effective leaders? What about Franklin D. Roosevelt and Mahatma Ghandi? Both these individuals have been identified by Burns (1978), by Bennis and Nanus (1985), and by others as successful leaders. But, was FDR's honesty and integrity substantially higher than that of everyone else? Of what business did Ghandi have intimate knowledge? Further, when did scholars who identified these traits know they were measuring the traits of leaders? Did the identification of leaders take place first by virtue of position or of success, or did a comprehensive measurement of traits indicate who might be correctly evaluated as a leader? The answer, of course, is that great people doing great things who are assumed to have great abilities were studied to discover what traits they possessed under the further assumption that what they were doing was necessarily leadership. On lower levels, anyone who supervises the work of others in an organization is frequently assumed to be doing leadership.

In the first four pages of their book, in or around a section proposing a "new theory" of leadership, Bennis and Nanus (1985) identified 22 historic figures as great leaders. Like many others, Bennis and Nanus defined leadership by defining abilities, characteristics, and activities of the leader. On page five, they stated flatly that the great man theories of leadership failed to explain leadership, but throughout their book they used CEOs and famous people as examples of good leadership.

Bass (1990), in the eighth section of his tome, acknowledged new paradigms in leadership thinking:

> Recent developments in the mathematics of dealing with irregularities, reversals in trends, and seemingly chaotic conditions may be applied to modeling the natural discontinuities in leader-follower relationships. The physical sciences may suggest new ways of looking at short-lived phenomena, for example, the emergence of instant leadership in a crisis followed by its equally instant disappearance. The willingness to accept two distinctive ways of dealing with the same phenomenon, as is common in wave and particle physics, may lead leadership theorists to treat simultaneously the leader's and subordinates' different rationales for what is happening. Cause-and-effect analysis may be seen as the exception to mutual interactions between leader and group outcomes (p. 882).

Following this rather close encounter with the metaphysics of science, Bass declared "in the new paradigm, the transformational leader moved the followers to transcend their own interests for the good of the group, organization, or society . . . transformational leaders, like charasmatics, attract strong feelings of identification from their subordinates" (p. 902). Bass presented this statement as the view for the Twenty-First Century. His statement of "the new paradigm" still clings to the idea that leadership is about leaders supervising subordinates, about subordinates working hard toward institutional objectives as the primary goal for leadership, and about the leader's ability to persuade/inspire/motivate subordinates to release their own needs and to work toward the interests of the leader or of the institution that the leader represents.

Another golden opportunity to examine conventional knowledge of the study of leadership and to explore the new paradigm was handed to Yukl and Van Fleet (1992). In the second edition of Marvin Dunnette's *Handbook of Industrial and Organizational Psychology*, Yukl and Van Fleet wrote the section on theory and research in leadership. They began the section with an overview of the literature, with "an emphasis on recent trends and developments likely to dominate the field through the turn of the century" (p. 148). They acknowledged that "some theorists believe that leadership is inherent in the social influence processes occurring among members of a group or organization, and leadership is a collective process shared among the members" (p. 148). But they chose to adopt the view "that all groups have role specialization, including a specialized leadership role wherein one person has more influence than other members and carries out some leadership functions that cannot be shared without jeopardizing the success of the group's mission" (p. 148).

The implication of the view adopted by Yukl and Van Fleet is that the group's mission is the same as organizational objectives. If the mission was truly created and understood by group members as their own, all group members could be trusted to pursue it without jeopardy, regardless of the leader's orientation or influence. While it is possible for the group to develop its own mission, little discussion was devoted to that possibility. The leader was assumed to be the source of the group's mission, and the source of motivation among group members to pursue this mission. This assumption regarding the source of mission determines whether research will center on the attributes, skills, abilities, and actions of a single leader carrying out assignments, or on reciprocal influence processes and integrative functions performed by a variety of people in the organization.

Yukl and Van Fleet's response to the general criticism of scholars who do not define leadership was the following: "Definitions are somewhat arbitrary, and controversies about the best way to define leadership usually cause confusion and animosity rather than providing new insights into the nature of the process. At this point in the development of the field, it is not necessary to resolve the controversy over the appropriate definition of leadership" (p. 149). So, rather than causing confusion and animosity, the authors chose to present the "theories" developed over the past century and the best way to validate those theories though research methodology without defining the *thing* that is being studied. This position is taken even though the studies they cited were clearly conducted under the assumption that leadership is some qualified ability to supervise or to manipulate people. If definitions are arbitrary, it is only because they have not been developed or supported.

Despite their reluctance to cause controversy, Yukl and Van Fleet offered this as an undeveloped definition: "Leadership is viewed as a process that includes influencing the task objectives and strategies of a group or organization, influencing people in the organization to implement the strategies and achieve the objectives, influencing group maintenance and identification, and influencing the culture of the organization" (p. 149). The authors added that they will use the terms *leadership* and *management* interchangeably throughout their discussion without reference to the various arguments that they are different *things* to define and to study. While these authors use the word *process*, it is clear that they are still referring to the leader's *ability* to create and to maintain influence. Therefore, the "new" theory of leadership, according to Yukl and Van Fleet, is founded on the assumption that leadership is all about the leader's ability to influence people to perform tasks and to implement strategies to, as Rost (1991) has nicely put it, do the leader's wishes, and that leadership is the same as management. This view of leadership is entirely conventional, and not new.

The most recent books and articles on leadership claiming to offer new perspectives generally do not show much deviation from convention. Most books with the word *leadership* in the title are either self-help books, promoting self-efficacy labeled as leadership, or pop management books that agree with Yukl and Van Fleet that leadership and management are the same thing. For example, the book *Virtual Leadership*, by Kostner (1994) is a novel about a modern *project leader* who is charged with extracting performance out of a geographically distributed work team. He is mentored by "the most legendary multi-site leader of all time--King Arthur of Camelot" (p. 1), and achieves business success upon the advice of a medieval king. While the book has many valuable management insights, it is a paragon of feudal wisdom, and provides nothing beyond conventional thinking on leadership.

Leadership and the New Science by Wheatley (1994) fulfills its promise of an application of the new science, but the application is directed toward management. The word *leadership* is rarely mentioned outside the title, much less defined.

More typical is a book edited by Shelton (1997), entitled *A New Paradigm of Leadership*, that contains fifty four sections written by different authors--some well-known leadership scholars, some practitioners. Each section is a collection of tips on how to manage organizations, and how to get employees to do what the boss wants them to do to achieve higher levels of performance. No section offers a definition of leadership.

Scholastic journal articles tend to follow the same line of conventional thinking. Sparrowe and Liden (1997) insisted that "leaders form different types of exchange relationships with their subordinates" (p. 522). Leader-Member Exchange Theory (LMX), as exemplified in this article, is focused on the ability of the leader to extract member performance by skillful exchange of valued things. The focus of this article is on exchange behavior relative to job assignments. While leadership is not defined, leaders are characterized as those who socialize and orient members in the ways of institutional needs.

A discussion of *international leadership* by Peterson and Hunt (1997) focused on international and multicultural perceptions of leaders and heros. While the discussion raises some important issues regarding the generalization of what is largely ethnocentric social science conducted in the US, there is no basis presented for a definition of leadership, and leadership is assumed to be a function of how leaders conduct themselves in different cultural settings.

Pawar and Eastman (1997) claim in the title of their article to be providing a conceptual examination of transformational leadership, but they limit their discussion to the top level of the organization and to the CEO's ability to create and to manage change. Leadership is not defined, but is characterized as a mechanism for accomplishing goals: "The transformational leader effects organizational change through the articulation of the leader's vision, the acceptance of the vision by followers, and the creation of a congruence between followers' self-interests and the vision" (p. 82). The successful transformational leader finds a way to convince followers to align their self-interests and subsequent actions with organizational structure and goals.

One approach to leadership study that initially appeared promising was the formulation of *democratic leadership* by Kurt Lewin (1950).

Lewin was attempting to establish a substantive distinction among authoritarian leadership, democratic leadership, and laissez-faire management. Unfortunately, Lewin and his colleagues ended their exploration with leader style, as a characteristic of the leader, and seem to have done more to define management than to define leadership. And, as Rost (1991) has argued, authoritarian leadership is not leadership. That leaves democratic leadership as the only road to the study of leadership. But, subsequent exploration of that idea has been confounded by the need for measurable variables even though it has popular support by those who value democracy.

A more comprehensive explanation of democratic leadership was conducted by Gastil (1994). Gastil adopted Lewin's central idea that democratic leadership is the outcome of the influence of the leader's behavior on people in a manner consistent with democratic principles. Gastil's elaboration of this idea included the relationship between authority and leadership, the functions of democratic leadership, the distribution of leadership, the roles of democratic followers, and the appropriate settings for democratic leadership. Aside from the old assumptions that leadership is an ability of the leader, in this case the ability to persuade, and that democratic leadership is one of many styles that can be applied or not by choice, there is some ancient baggage that prevents this idea from being viable as a process explanation of leadership outcomes.

Ancient Greece was the birthplace of modern administrative thinking, and specifically associated with democracy. As discussed in the third chapter, Aristotle was skeptical of the value of democracy as a viable form of government because it creates too many variables and varied influences on the decision process to facilitate efficient running of the state. Before Aristotle, Plato had implanted the idea that democracy is dangerous because the hegemony of demos would disrupt all classes of society (Takala, 1998). Aristotle made the point that if a democratic state were made up of ten thousand fools and five geniuses, every vote would be ten thousand to five, and all in the wrong direction.

Plato was certain that a class structure in society with a ruling class of philosopher-kings would be the preferable alternative. Democracy invites change that Plato felt would interfere with the structure of society and would threaten the continuity of justice. As a counter to Athenian democracy as it existed, Plato promoted the transcendental abilities of the philosopher-king, who is possessed of magical skills and of superhuman wisdom. In short, by emphasizing traits and abilities, industrial leadership theory, even that of democratic (style) leadership, is still attempting to make a case for Plato's philosopher-king.

The Social Construct of Leadership

What do practioners think leadership is? Given that scholars routinely do not define it, one might assume that there is a consistent leadership construct or myth among the general population. An informal survey of 110 managers, administrators, and professionals of various ethnic backgrounds who worked for various public and private organizations in the Mid-Hudson region of New York State was conducted by the author in various settings, none of which had any direct links to the study of leadership. Participants were asked to complete (in writing) the following sentence: "leadership is a(n) ..."

Fifty nine respondents (54%) defined leadership as a skill or ability. Six defined it as a role or position. Thirteen (12%) defined it as an action. Another 13 offered no definition at all; that is, they wrote what leadership is about or what it relates to or what it is concerned with, but not what it is. The remaining respondents suggested that it is a responsibility, a weapon, a process, a function of management, a factor, a lifestyle, or an experience. Three suggested that it is an influencing relationship.

One might expect more consistency from students of the subject. A post hoc survey was conducted by the author on the final exams of 181 undergraduate students in an organizational behavior class who responded to an item specifically asking them to define leadership. Even though the text used in the class defined leadership as an ability, only 89 students (49%) defined it that way. Students were exposed to other definitions and encouraged to think of their own, but thirty two (18%) did not define leadership directly at all. The remaining definitions fell into categories similar to the ones listed above. Although it can be argued that these were not good students in the sense that they did not assimilate the information in the text or in the lectures, many of them may have relied upon their general social beliefs about leadership, therefore statement of the construct is similar for both samples.

Rost (1991) completed a thorough analysis of the theories, origins, and uses of the word *leadership*. He concluded that the words used to define leadership are contradictory, the models are discrepant, and the content of leadership is confused with the nature of leadership. For example, Gastil (1994) suggested that leaders can help to develop followers' emotional maturity and moral reasoning abilities, but then went on to admonish leaders to not become substitute parents. How does one address the emotional maturity and moral reasoning of others without becoming parental? And more broadly, if leadership is conceptualized as a theory of supervision--that is as a set of abilities or activities that have as their goal getting others to do what the leader wants them to do (which is not necessarily Gastil's view)--then why do leadership scholars not study parents? Is it because parents do not occupy a certain position in an organizational or social hierarchy? Is it because parents are not likely to pay for leadership books and seminars? The problem with the social construct of leadership is, as Rost and Burns have suggested, a focus upon the leader rather than upon leadership. Is leadership all about a position, about an ability, about a relationship, or about a process?

Consider the word *leadership* itself. Other words that end in the suffix *-ship* can be used to denote a skill, such as in the words *statesmanship, seamanship, brinkmanship,* or *craftsmanship.* These words are often characterized by the letters *man* which precede the suffix *-ship.* This suffix can also be used to indicate a relationship, as in *partnership, musicianship, apprenticeship, fellowship,* and in the word *relationship* itself. It seems there is a legitimate semantic choice to use words like *musicianship* or *leadership* either to indicate an ability or skill, or to indicate a form of relationship. An argument can be made that *leadermanship,* used to indicate a skill, is awkward and internally redundant. How leadership is defined, therefore, is related to how its definition is intended to be used.

Leadership As An Ability

As cited above, leadership is often defined in terms of the leader's ability to do something: to communicate effectively, to motivate subordinates, to bargain, to inspire, to mobilize, to transform, etc. A reading of articles in virtually any issue of the *Leadership Quarterly* finds, with rare exception, every article focused on leader abilities, traits, or behaviors. For example, transformational leadership is normally advocated as an effective method for manipulating followers: "transformational leaders encourage charismatically-led followers to develop their skills so that they might eventually demonstrate initiative in working for the leader's goals" (Graham, 1991, p. 116). This concept is clearly not consistent with Burns' (1978) definition of transforming leadership as a relationship, but is consistent with the view of leadership as a skill or an ability.

Focus on the leader's abilities and traits serves two important social functions: hope for salvation and blame for failure. The leader has been likened to "a saviorlike essence in a world that constantly needs saving" (Rost, 1991, p. 94), and leadership to a "social delusion that allows 'followers' to escape responsibility for their own actions and inactions" (Gemmill & Oakley, 1992, p. 119). Rost contended that the popular view of leadership has its foundations in Hollywood, folkloric, and Old West images of what men do as leaders. Gemmill and Oakley viewed leadership as a myth, the major function of which is to preserve the existing social systems and structures by blaming the problems on inadequate leadership abilities and not on the systems themselves.

There is a certain value in focusing on the abilities and characteristics of leaders, particularly when developing a leadership training program for consumption. It is relatively easy to develop the seven steps of this or the ten ways of that, and to present these ways and steps very effectively. But as every trainer who has done so, and who is candid, will attest, the value of these ways and steps rarely finds its way beyond the classroom. What sounds good in the training seminar may not translate well into practice. The problem of translation is based in the gap between the simplistic statements of the ways and steps, and the complexities of social and organizational processes that comprise the context within which these skills and abilities must be carried out.

The efficacy of leadership training that focuses on abilities is doubtful because, even if the abilities, behavior, and characteristics of successful leaders could be identified, people generally cannot assimilate them without changing their personalities and their world views (Rost, 1993). Fleishman et al. (1991) listed 499 dimensions of leader behavior from 65 different systems. Naturally, many dimensions were repeated. Are individuals required to manifest all these dimensions before becoming leaders? One system had 23 dimensions. Even if a trainer were sincere about training leaders to enhance their abilities, and focused upon this one system, how could that be accomplished? Further, as Rost (1993) pointed out, how do the abilities of an effective leader within any of these systems differ from the abilities of an effective manager, or an effective person?

Management As An Ability

When we think of the ability of leaders, we are probably thinking of the ability of leaders to *manage*. Management, as an activity, is the mobilization and allocation of resources toward the accomplishment of specific goals. Mobilizing and allocating resources is a specific skill. Management includes the tasks of goal setting, strategic and operational planning, providing structure, organizing and directing the activities of others, motivating others to pursue organizational goals, manipulating and controlling outcomes and organizational systems, setting standards and measuring performance to standard, and making money for owners. In alluding back to the analogy of the ship, we can understand management as that which is applied to the steering mechanism. The direction of the ship is the result, in part, of that application; however, there are many other forces to consider. For example, if the engine is not running, the direction of the ship is determined primarily by outside forces no matter how efficient the application of management to the steering.

Everyone is a manager to some degree. Everyone has specific personal objectives and personal resources. Managers in organizations differ from individuals who manage themselves in that the self-manager does not usually create structure or supervise the work of others (the management functions of *organizing* and *directing*). Self-managers plan, set goals, mobilize resources, and establish controls to monitor performance and to correct errors. The management function of *directing* has specifically to do with supervising the work of others to accomplish goals. People are resources. So the acts of setting goals and of getting people to do things to achieve those goals are functions of management. Some authors replace the word *directing* with the word *leading* as the third function of management. That would make leading a subset of management, and most certainly an activity of supervision. If that is true, why not simply define leadership and supervision as the same thing, or better yet, abandon the word *leadership* and get on with research into effective supervision?

Success in management can be directly attributed to an ability to carry out the various functions of management. Success in management is moderated by the situation. The management abilities of a given person are more effective under certain circumstances, less effective under others. Management abilities can be learned within the context of a given individual's personality, can be improved with practice, and can be applied with a given style. Certainly, most discussions of *leadership* are really discussions of management with an attempt to elevate the status of the manager to the level of Plato's philosopher-king. Specifically, managers rely upon two important abilities: the ability to supervise, and the ability to persuade which we may call *statesmanship*. These abilities and their role in the leadership relationship will be discussed further in Chapter Six.

The fundamental difference between leadership and management lies in their respective roles in organizations and in society. The role of leadership is to create change while the role of management is to create stability. Stability is created by managing routine, incremental, and continuous change through planning, organizing, directing, controlling, and effective staffing. The purpose of management is to stabilize the activities of the organization by maintaining successful patterns of action through the development and control of standard operating procedures. Strategic or social change can be chaotic. Strategic change is often nonroutine, nonincremental, and discontinuous change which alters the structure and overall orientation of the organization or its components (Tichy, 1983). Strategic change often stimulates leadership by creating new patterns of action and new belief systems. Management protects stabilized patterns and beliefs. The function of management regarding change is to anticipate change and to adapt to it, but not to create it.

Management is primarily a rational activity. Rational methods are particularly useful for creating and for maintaining stability. The manager views the organization as a mechanistic system which can be controlled and adjusted through the acquisition and analysis of information. Inefficient or failing organizational systems are presumed to be losing energy because there is chaos somewhere in the system. To fix the problem, the manager finds a way to remove the chaos and to restore order to the system. Problem solving is therefore a rational process of defining the problem, generating and selecting alternatives, and implementing and evaluating the solution. The system is objective, predictable, and controllable through the acquisition and analysis of information about the system and its workings. Skills training, particularly in problem solving, is very effective when focused upon the rational activities of management.

The view of leadership as management ability is the basis of the industrial paradigm of leadership. This paradigm relies upon the simplistic concept of the leader as a giver of direction and as a manipulator of will, who frames and solves specific management or social problems. Like the feudal paradigm, the industrial paradigm has its application. It defines and resolves a number of issues that can result from the need for an imposed order and from the need to accomplish specific goals.

The limitations of the industrial paradigm of leadership are apparent when the goals are not specific, or when the imposition of order does not solve the problem. These limitations become more evident as social issues, structures, and problems become more complex. A recognition of the emerging need for a more appropriate paradigm is what likely led Burns (1978) to explore a view of transforming leadership that accommodates complex social and political processes.

But like all paradigm shifts, the new perspective has been slow to take hold, and is commonly interpreted by those who steadfastly cling to the old paradigm as simply an extension of their old views. For example, the concept of transformational leadership described by Bass (1990) and others clearly borrowed the label from Burns but still relies upon the traits and abilities of the leader to transform a lackluster organization into a profitable enterprise through the manipulation of employees' motives. This application measures leadership by performance to goals. These goals usually represent a symbolic acquisition of territory: return on investment, market share, or diversification. What if the goal is freedom, education, social development, or some other end-value? What if the problem is racism or drug abuse? Success is not so simple to define and to measure. The conventional theories of leadership are simply inadequate explanations of any approach to resolving these problems.

Chapter 5

Leadership as a Process

Leadership must necessarily be understood relative to social processes and to the structure of the society that people take action to create, to maintain, and to change. As stated in Chapter Two, the relationship between action and structure is mitigated by what Giddens (1982) called *the duality of structure*. Structural properties of social systems are both medium and outcomes of the practices and activities that comprise those systems. Social processes are like rivers, flowing within and shaping their own beds at the same time. The complex, reciprocal relationships of people and institutions, then, must be the foci of the explanation of leadership. The duality of structure ultimately connects that which constitutes the leader and that which creates outcomes in a way that cannot be explained by simply defining the abilities of the leader or defining any dyadic relationship between the leader and a given subordinate.

There is a difference between what we have defined as leadership and what we experience as leadership (Rost, 1991). Burns (1978) expressed the belief that the experience of leadership is centered about a striving to satisfy our mutual wants and needs. A construct of leadership can be built upon a direct, phenomenological experience of leadership that occurs prior to the creation or adaptation of conventional knowledge about it. Using Pirsig's (1991) Metaphysics of Quality, as mentioned in Chapter One, this experience can be assessed through value preferences. As opposed to the view, for example, that leader authenticity causes morale, one can hold the view that participants in the leadership process prefer a precondition of authenticity, which, when present, may provide a context that allows for their morale to increase. These participants may potentially move in some other direction if their morale (*eudaimonia*) is energized by some other value.

The question for leadership study is *what motivates people to modify their self-interest and work collectively toward common goals?* The conventional answer is to identify the leader as the source of motivation, or if not the source, at least the stimulus. The leader is thought to inspire work toward a vision of ends, or to stimulate work toward an objective through the ability to exchange valued things, or simply to bring about outcomes by threat of punishment.

In Chapter Two, the suggestion was made that people are motivated by a potential for *eudaimonia*--the enjoyment and fulfillment one experiences when doing something presumed to be of *consequence*. While *eudaimonia* is a desired outcome for the individual relative to some understanding of *telos*, *telos* itself is a collective ideal that is related to other collective ideas about wants and needs. The simple answer to the question, therefore, is that *eudaimonia* motivates people to modify their self-interest to work collectively toward *our telos*. Unfortunately, this answer amounts to little more than a statement of the obvious, and tells us nothing about leadership except in what way it is collective.

The key to understanding *eudaimonia* as a motivator is found in the presumption of *consequence*. *Consequence* cannot be simply defined, designated, or assigned by the leader; it must be presumed and understood by the actor. Industrial theories of leadership seem to at least incorporate that understanding, but tend to overstate and to oversimplify the leader's role in organizing and influencing the actor's presumptions of *consequence*.

When groups of people interact there are necessarily conflicting values because people, having been affected by the social order and by personal history in different ways, each have a somewhat different summum bonum--a concept of what is needed to produce a continuous state of *eudaimonia*. The process that aligns these individual ethics toward a shared summum bonum (*our telos*) is the phenomenon often experienced as leadership. Leadership is a means for individuals to explore, to understand, to modify, and to articulate their own ethics, and to compare them with the ethics of other individuals. Through the leadership process, people come to visualize a *telos*, that in turn highlights the parameters of *eudaimonia*, that in turn comes to be manifested in leadership role expectations, which in turn come to be symbolized by and attributed to the leader. It is not the leader who creates leadership, it is leadership that creates the leader.

The process of leadership is stimulated by some perceived differential between what people collectively want and what they currently have. When that differential is large enough, or critical enough, it motivates people to act. Through influencing, compromising, and sacrificing, members of a community create a vision (specifically a common image) of a future good--that is, a new moral order that accommodates their collective wants and needs. Such things as capturing a certain market share, or generating a return on investment of twenty percent, do not represent a vision, but a goal. These sorts of things rarely stimulate the leadership process because too few individuals in a community of workers are likely to see them as consequential. Such things are rarely understood as a collective good by more than a handful of people, whose interest in them usually has more to do with the accumulation of money than with *eudaimonia.*

From a truly collective vision are created (or modified) the community mores which define behavioral standards, role expectations, and contractual commitments (justice) from which ultimate goals--even ROI and market share--are pursued and realized. The shared vision is shared because it is *our telos,* and because it is the outgrowth of social processes that we experience together. A *vision* is not simply the product of one individual or small group who decided upon a goal or sold an idea. The collective good is collective because it is inextricably linked with every individual's summum bonum and with the human condition as understood within a particular social reality. That is what is meant by the word *mutual.* The *telos* of a group of employees in an organization cannot be to increase the wealth of the owners through hard or efficient work unless they themselves *are* the owners, or unless they see the increase of wealth or the activity itself as something of *consequence. Our telos* could also possibly include making the lives of the organization's owners (our oppressors) as miserable as possible.

Leadership is necessarily founded in crisis. It is crisis that acts as a catalyst for the leadership process. For this purpose, crisis can be defined as a perceived differential between what exists in the social order and what is desired by an individual that is strong enough to be motivating. Crisis is an individual perception that can be perceived in the same way by many individuals at the same time, or differently by different individuals. Crisis orients people to begin to think about change. The crisis of September 11, 2001 stimulated many changes that certain *leaders* had been advocating for years without successfully bringing them about. Crisis gives people incentive to consider actions, trade-offs, and sacrifices that they would not have considered otherwise. Communities in crisis are usually more unified toward a community objective than communities in peace time.

Because it is largely an uncontrollable process, leadership that occurs within an organization in serious trouble may result in unpredictable and undesirable outcomes. If the ship's engine has too much power for the design or capacity of the hull, the steering mechanisms will not work in optimal or in predictable ways. The vessel itself may come apart. Leadership that happens spontaneously within an organization can be extremely disruptive to the management process. On the other hand, if employees pull together as a community during a time of crisis, they can work miracles even if they act in contradiction with the rational management of the organization. Again, if managers try to manipulate a group of employees, by whatever means, to carry out objectives that are not *mutually* created, the result is an authority/supervisory relationship in which power is exercised and it is not leadership. The differences between an authority relationship and a leadership relationship will be discussed in greater detail in the next chapter.

Once leadership is understood as a dynamic social process with multiple actors who are pursuing mutual ends, it makes sense to remove references to the leader altogether. Leadership was defined by Wren (1995) as "an influence process whereby group members seek to adapt successfully to challenges to shared purposes and the common good" (p. 135). In this view of leadership, the leader only symbolizes, or at most facilitates, the process of adaptation.

The year before September 11, 2001, Rudy Giuliani, Mayor of New York City, had trouble mobilizing enough support for a senatorial campaign. After September 11th he was a national hero, not because he was a different person with new *leadership skills* and with a different *vision*, but because his usual approach to problem solving represented accurately how people collectively felt about what needed to be done to adapt to this new reality. Adaptation implies that leadership is among the most fundamental of human activities, that which insures survival.

Because humans are social creatures, the adaptation of any one individual is facilitated by the adaptation of all. Then, the means of adaptation must be shared by some critical mass of a society's members. But the common good is more than simply a utilitarian approach to adaptation. The common good is an ideal that embraces desired improvements to the human condition. Leadership can be a process of adaptation and survival, but it is also the process people use to challenge the existing order, and to pursue these improvements. A value for improvement provides the motivation needed to challenge the status quo.

To understand this challenge, the relationship between the moral order and motivation to behave must be addressed. While morals are express adaptations of behavior to social and environmental conditions, ethics have to do with individual ideas about improvements to the human condition and about the search for meaning. The leadership process is strong and aligned when there is a common understanding of what changes are needed for the common good. The leadership process is weak or non-existent when ethics are diverse, when there is no common sense of *our telos*, when there is no strong desire to change the moral order, and when people have dramatically different ideas about what constitutes an improvement.

The community is the arena of leadership not only because of the role of the moral order in motivation and in transformation, but because the community itself is an outcome of the desire for association. People need to be a part of something greater than themselves. Some degree of any given individual's identity originates in a social group with which the individual shares some set of values. Ethics are the magnets for the formation of communities, and provide the compass for the direction of the community and for the common good. Therefore, the study of ethics as individual orientations must be a central and unifying theme for leadership study.

Morals are merely outcomes of collective actions that people take to pursue *eudaimonia*: "Man is never driven to moral behavior; in each instance he decides to behave morally" (Frankl, 1969, p. 158). Ethics are guides in the search for meaning. "Man's search for meaning is a primary force in his life and not a 'secondary rationalization' of instinctive drives" (Frankl, 1969, p. 154). People live and die for the sake of their values and ideals. Ethics are essential elements of leadership because they involve much more than what is represented by self-interest. "If the meaning that is waiting to be fulfilled by man were really nothing but a mere expression of self, or no more than a projection of wishful thinking, it would immediately lose its demanding and challenging character; it could no longer call man forth or summon him" (Frankl, 1969, p. 156). Ethics must be understood as the essential motivating forces fueling the will of participants to work together toward some ultimate end in the leadership process.

The Moral Order as a Context for Leadership

The constitution of a *polis*, as discussed by Aristotle, is only one element of the society's moral order. Social groups may have multiple constitutions (that is, multiple states or organizations), or have no constitution (no recognizable *polis*) at all. The moral order of a society contains the rules and customs that govern behavior and theory about behavior, even if it is not organized into a constitution. A constitution is a specific and consensual determinant of governance and of governing structure, while the moral order represents a psychological map of the society. Constitutions are subject to change through conscious and deliberate processes of negotiating, bargaining, and influencing, while the moral order is shaped through largely subconscious, habitual behavior that is generally not intended to institute change. The moral order is ultimately shaped and reshaped by the collective behavioral patterns of the individual members of the culture, so the duality of structure must be taken into account in any form of social analysis. Therefore, no social context can be assumed to follow linear patterns. Before leadership can be understood in the context of the *polis*, it must be understood in the context of the moral order.

Analysis of the context of leadership has been confounded by the same reductionism that has confounded physical science. Physical science is thought to be understandable only if all phenomena are reduced to the same level of inquiry (Jantsch, 1980). Reductionism depends upon a spacial structure where pieces can be disassembled and then reassembled. The structure is understood when key relationships among various combinations of components or subsystems are discovered. This view assumes that microsystems are simply subsystems of macrosystems, and that the latter is an unchanging *environment* of the former. In order to make sense of microsystems, the macrosystem must be static or stable. If the macrosystem changes, microsystems are disrupted. If key relationships within a microsystem are influenced by change in the macrosystem, they become different relationships.

Hunt (1991) purported to offer a new synthesis--an extended model--of leadership. His discussion focused upon an analysis of the context of leadership, but developed no foundation for a definition. Given the context, leadership was divided into three domains: systems leadership (top level), organizational leadership (intermediate level), and direct leadership (bottom level). The extensive analysis of "immensely complex environmental and societal--culture/values forces facing leaders at the highest levels" (p. 27) accounted for three levels of differing complexity, but did not employ a metaphysical framework sufficient to organize an understanding of the differences among the domains. Domains were taken to be established by the complexity of the jobs held by supervisors at each level, and differences were implied to be related more to the status of the activity than to the nature of the activity.

In a large sense, Hunt's discussion of the context was bounded by perceptions of the leader as the source of leadership, and by an understanding of the context as a multi-leveled obstacle with which the leader must cope. Indeed, chapter six was devoted to the individual background factors (traits) and capabilities needed by leaders to cope with contextual issues. Supervisors are thought to cope with the simplest level, managers with the intermediate level of complexity, and executives with the highest level. This assignment of complexity implies in a conventional way that executives know more than other people do, and are therefore worth the extra money.

If social processes are less complex at lower levels of the organization, it is probably because they are merely seen that way by the observer. How, for example, is the executive's task of interpreting the dynamics of the marketplace more complex than the supervisor's task of interpreting the dynamics of executive decision making, or the dynamics of employee resistance to change? Potentially, information is more readily available about the market than about internal management decisions because upper level managers tend to hoard information to protect their self-interests (Jackall, 1988). Hunt's discussion of the complexity of the context would have been enhanced by an ontological foundation, something that would establish a differentiation among his domains in a way that explains the interactions they have with the macrosystem.

Leader-centered theories of leadership, such as Hunt's, are reductionistic; the leader represents a microsystem, and the task is to explain the nature of the leader--disassembling and reassembling the leader, if you will. The *environment* of leadership, then, is some form of social milieu, such as a society, an industry, a market, an organization, or a small group that has specific influences upon how the leader formulates leadership. These theories depend for their integrity on stable and consistent measurements of both the macro and micro systems; relationships among system components (traits, abilities, actions, etc.) are presumed to be established and to be activated within a stable environment. A change in the environment would require new definitions (or at least reverification) of these relationships.

Social systems are not static systems, and not likely to remain stable for long periods of time. To begin with, people in a large social system can influence each other even if they never meet, and if they have no knowledge of each other's existence. An accounting of this form of relationship is not possible by traditional measurements of group parameters. In addition, not all properties of macrosystems necessarily follow from the properties of their subsystems or components--it cannot be stated that outcomes in society or in an organization are necessarily properties of leadership, or of supervision, or of management. Rather, some properties of macrosystems are the result of dynamic interactions with subsystems; they change at the same time, and sometimes in unpredictable ways. Reductionism does not account for these dynamic interactions. Therefore, studies of social processes must be approached upon different levels of inquiry. Jantsch (1980) distinguished three levels of inquiry that are irreducible to each other: (a) classical or Newtonian dynamics, (b) an equilibrium-seeking systems model based in laws of thermodynamics, and (c) dissipative structures.

Newtonian science operates under assumptions of purity and exclusivity--behavior can be isolated and studied without reference to other entities. It is this view of systems that has predominated leadership studies in particular, and management theory and social science in general. The universe (macrosystem) and all of its subsystems are thought to be stable, orderly, and predictable. Control of the system or organization is presumed to be attained through the measurement of phenomena and the prediction of change. Change can be made predictable even if it is not mechanistic because it can be minimized or incrementalized through measurement and control. Leadership, within this view of change, is characterized as mechanistic, linear, predictable, and subject to definition through numeric constants. The stability of the classical system (as applied to organizations) is accomplished through the imposition of structure and standard operating procedures that are assumed to provide the organization with stability and the leader with control. The classical system has been applied to management and to theories of administration by Weber (1947), Taylor (1911), and others and is popular because it provides some degree of certainty for managers.

A thermodynamic system is always evolving toward a state of equilibrium, which in turn provides the sole reference point for defining the system. The origin and extinction of an equilibrium-seeking system are determined by some degree of disruption which causes the system to change energy levels. A key concept used to understand change in energy levels in a thermodynamic system is *entropy*. Entropy is a complex idea that is used to explain the conservation of energy. Thermodynamic systems increase their entropy when they lose energy, or when energy becomes unavailable for work. In organizations, entropy can result from disruption, and sources of entropy are sought out by managers for correction.

The equilibrium-seeking, or structure-preserving, organization is one in which certainty and stability are important goals, but complete stability or control is not expected because some degree of change that will result in energy loss is understood as either unpredictable or uncontrollable. Spurts of dynamic change are thought to be contained within predictable patterns of variation. Rather than in linear control, leadership is assumed to be centered in some form of stable or predictable oscillation, such as in social, economic, or market cycles. For this type of system, unpredictable change (loss of energy) is assumed to be continuous, and is met by managers with adaptation and with reorientation. Managers tend to assume that change is incremental in nature, and that adaptation or minimizing energy loss can be facilitated through sequential shifting of structure.

A dissipative (transforming or chaotic) system is defined by a "spontaneous formation of structures in open systems which exchange energy and matter with their environment" (Jantsch, 1980, p. 26). There are three characteristics: (1) they are open to the environment, (2) they are far from equilibrium, and (3) they necessarily include autocatalytic steps. The dissipative system can release entropy to its environment, and can dissipate or self-energize. The *accounting* for entropy must include the environment. The environment changes with the microsystem in a mutually influencing way. The *structure* of a dissipative system is not a solid, tangible structure, but a process structure--what Jantsch referred to as a dynamic régime.

Technically, chaotic systems can only be defined statistically by identifying discontinuous collections of data points on a graph, called strange attractors (Kiel, 1994). The presence of strange attractors signals that the system is chaotic and not random. As applied to leadership or to theories of management and administration, chaos theory should be understood as metaphorical and not statistical. Still, the term *chaos* can be misleading. One application of chaos theory to management is deterministic, in the sense of classical and thermodynamic models. This view provides managers with answers to problems and with methods for finding those answers. Another view is what Overman (1996) called *quantum administration*. The quantum view holds that reality emerges from a perception of the changing order, and that what managers do to obtain an answer will influence the nature of the answer. "Quantum administration is a world with different foci: on energy, not matter; on becoming, not being; on coincidence, not causes; on constructivism, not determinism; and on new states of awareness and consciousness" (p. 489).

Chaos theory is the study of complex, deterministic, nonlinear, dynamic systems (Kellert, 1993). Dissipative or transforming change is very complex, very dynamic, and necessarily discontinuous. A system is transforming when the existing structures of the system dissipate and transform into new forms or structures. Within this dynamic system, there is an internal capacity to reconfigure in response to gradual or to sudden change whether it is predicted or not. This internal capacity is not necessarily correlated with any given set of consistently identifiable or measurable variables. A dissipative system continuously renews itself within a dynamic context without any a priori goal.

Rather than seeking to preserve its structure in some form as the classical and equilibrium-seeking systems do, the transforming system evolves into new modes of operation, new orders of structure, and new relationships with its environment. Reorganizing a hierarchical (organizational) structure into a new hierarchy is not necessarily a transformation. If an ant hill were leveled and a new one built by the ants, the result is not a transformation but merely a structure-preserving adaptation to change by rebuilding using the same structural knowledge. Two key differences that distinguish the transforming system are that this system (a) is not organized by strategic, rational thought, and (b) responds to change not as a disruptive irregularity, but as an integral element of the environment. If the ants sprouted wings and moved to the trees instead of rebuilding in the ground, that would be a transformation.

A quick illustration of the relationship of these three levels of inquiry to leader-centered views of leadership can be made by using the analogy of a person carrying a bowl of water. In the classical system, the leader's role is to minimize the disturbance or ripples in the bowl. In order to minimize ripples, the leader will change as little as possible to maximize control. There is an implicit assumption that the leader can isolate the elements of the system, avoid outside interference and disruptive change, and maintain stability through prediction and control.

A bowl of ripples is thought, within this view, to indicate an incompetent leader.

If the system is equilibrium-seeking, the leader's role then is to be reactionary and adaptive in nature--goal oriented, but driven to some extent by changing environmental demands, like a changing market or a changing technology. The equilibrium system is a deterministic system that is acknowledged to be subject to unavoidable and commonly unanticipated disturbances from outside (and perhaps from inside) the system. The person in charge must change to meet demands for action, but is still focused on stabilizing the system as much as possible because equilibrium is still considered to be the desired state of existence for the system. Here, our water carrier is moving rapidly to keep up, while being jostled from all sides, trying to minimize the amount of water lost from the bowl. An unacceptable level of loss will signal the extinction of the system, and is thought to indicate an incompetent leader.

In the transforming system, the leader's role cannot be defined in advance, but emerges from the dissipative or transforming processes. The bowl of water is expelled into the air, and whatever comes down is fundamentally and structurally different than what it was before; this is transformation. In the transforming system, there cannot be any form of standardized control, any theory of prediction, or any form of measurable constant (such as traits, structures, styles, and so forth) as determinants of leadership. In fact, in a transforming system, whatever we experience or measure as leadership is itself transforming as a part of the system; the macrosystem changes as a part of the transformation. Therefore, it makes little sense to discuss any constant quality of the leader as the source of leadership. While chaotic systems may be known and managed by way of experience (Overman, 1996), leadership in a transforming system may not be associated with any form of deliberate control or of preselected, specific goals for outcomes. Part of understanding chaos theory is perceiving organizational phenomena within new frameworks, and using a new language to order and to communicate those perceptions.

Imagine a carnival. The carnival itself is an equilibrium-seeking system, following predictable cycles: setting up, tearing down, and reforming in a different location, adapting its structure to different physical features and different audiences. But, the structure of the carnival provides an environment for the crowd that is transforming. There are various attractions set up in a structured way, but the crowd responds to the structure of the environment by creating, dissolving, and recreating its own structure. While the structure of the attractions (environment) has influence on the crowd, the crowd's patterns are primarily influenced by the direct application of value. From a single vantage point, the crowd appears chaotic sometimes and orderly other times. As different attractions change activity levels, lines form and then dissipate and then reform somewhere else.

Taken as a whole, the crowd appears to be a mass of people milling about randomly. But careful observation will reveal groupings of people waxing and waning in what may eventually become predictable patterns of structure. This predictability is not the result of a priori, cause/effect relationships, but emerges from collected observations of the results of applied values over time within a given context. The patterns formed at any one time eventually change in form, not mechanistically but organically; they do not shift, they bloom. The people in motion are reciprocally linked to the context within which they move, and their movement can adequately be explained only by referring to the values they apply to the choices of movement they make. The values governing movement of people in the crowd are energized to some extent by qualities of the environment: displays, music, activity, etc.

A ready example of the use of one level of inquiry when two levels would have been more appropriate can be found in Wills' (1994) discussion of *military leadership*. Wills used Napoleon as an example of a military leader, and George McClellan as an example of an antitype. Wills obviously assumed that any person holding the title of *General* must necessarily be assessed as a military leader. While Napoleon was clearly a good military combat general, McClellan did not satisfy anyone's definition of a combat general. McClellan was good at organizing the military and preparing it for combat. In fact, some historians have suggested that the success of the Army of the Potomac was due at least in part to McClellan's skill at preparation (Foote, 1958).

If any social context can be described as a linear system, military training fits that description. Military drills are very highly structured, as is military life in general. If any context can be described as a transforming system, combat can be, as any combat soldier will verify. Wills seems to have recognized the distinction between management from a classical system perspective and what leadership might be as experienced in a transforming system, yet he did not adopt a framework or a language suitable for conceptualizing or for explaining the difference. Leadership has much more to do with action based upon perceptions of emerging structure in systems where order is periodically breaking down and reforming than it does with the imposition of structure and control relative to an a priori configuration. The *leader* has no more influence on the emerging structure than the carnival barker has on the crowd.

At this point, it is possible to make a few tentative statements about the context of leadership:

(1) leadership is associated with a transforming or chaotic system and not with a classical or equilibrium-seeking system--leadership is not about control of the context;

(2) the context of leadership as a dissipative system is irreducible--knowing the system does not mean that its elements are known (Jantsch, 1980);

(3) the context of leadership is irreversible--progressive and not repetitive (Overman, 1996);

(4) the higher level order (strange attractors) that results in part from the duality of structure in the leadership process may be perceived only by a few individuals, and perhaps by no one at all;

(5) leadership, like perceived order, emerges from the system;

(6) microsystems, such as organizations or leaders themselves, exchange energy with their environment and cannot be understood apart from the macrosystem. Process and its associated structure form the vessel of leadership; chaos, complexity, and conflict are not problems to be solved, they are the engines of evolution, adaptation, and renewal that characterize leadership.

The Nature of Leadership

"To study the laws of history, we must completely change the subject of our observation, must leave aside kings, ministers, and generals, and study the common and infinitesimally small elements by which the masses are moved" (Tolstoy, 1952, p. 470). The infinitesimally small elements by which the masses are moved are their individual wills-- a compilation of their personal values and their needs, or more specifically their ethics. An ethic is a foundation of value that defines one's character and provides individuals with a sense of purpose and direction. Ethics are spiritual definitions of life that, for the individual, create and sustain motivation, and guide social action. The distinction between ethics and the moral systems in which ethics may be acted out-- between *my needs* and *society's needs*--is crucial to the understanding of the difference between energy and structure in social systems.

Leadership scholars have been searching for structures to predict and to control, and not for dynamic value (energy). Dynamic value in social processes is created by spontaneously varying combinations of individual values. Structures in society emerge from dynamic value, and may in turn be swallowed up again. The values of individuals influence collective values, which then reciprocate; ethics create mores, which in turn create ethics. People act to meet their own needs. An accretion of these actions formulates institutions, which have been created to meet individual needs. Dynamic change in a classical system is thought to be a deviation from normal static patterns, and becomes something to be dissected, explained, and controlled. But, in a self-organizing system, unpredicted and dynamic change is the essential component of the system, and the source of the conflict to which Burns was referring.

Although dissipative systems are largely unpredictable, they obey rules. Specifically, the rules are established through some principle of self-organization, and these rules create the internal consistency that differentiates chaotic systems from random behavior. These rules are not standard operating procedures as they are understood in a classic system. They are not rules devised to standardize outcomes. Rather, they are rules only by virtue of their consistent influence on patterns over time. They cannot be created, but they can be interpreted.

The basis for evolution within a dissipative social system is a balance between generation and degeneration moderated by a balance between deviation and convention. A potentially infinite number of deviations may be available in any given system. Deviations which take hold do so because they are consistent with the system's overall direction. After a time, patterns of deviation become convention.

One limitation imposed by traditional research methods in the study of industrial leadership is the reluctance of researchers to accept degeneration as an essential part of the system's behavior and development. The concept of degeneration as discussed by Machiavelli in *The Discourses* will be explored further as a context for leadership relationships in the next chapter. *Effective leadership* is thought to be associated only with growth, and not with decline. That which represents growth, or progress, is always defined by convention.

In industrial management, convention is held by a death-grip while deviation from convention is actively suppressed, minimized, avoided, or eliminated. Burns (1978) recognized the role of deviation in the evolution of the system, which he labeled conflict. Contrary to industrial management wisdom, the evolving transformative system must degenerate before it regenerates. Executives, such as Iacocca, are often given credit for turning around organizations that are in deep trouble. It is possible that what is perceived as trouble was the natural course of restructuring in an evolving dissipative system. The executive could be merely along for the ride. On the other hand, executives certainly have some degree of influence, probably a different degree in each case, upon which path the dissipation and subsequent regeneration will take.

Functions of a classic system are conceived as elements of the system designed to produce outcomes by regulating processes. The function of a dissipative system embraces its processes as they unfold. Generally speaking, the only function of a dissipative system is self-renewal. It has no object beyond that, and it can be a source of extreme frustration for those who would wish it in a certain direction. For example, if the global ecosystem is understood as a classic system, then the function of the system would be to support existing life, and the process of pollution is a deviation to be managed. If the ecosystem is understood as a dissipative system, then the function of the system is to evolve. Pollution is one outcome of internal system processes that will be adjusted when the system dissipates and then regenerates. Of course, its regeneration will probably eliminate the sources of pollution--specifically, human beings who cannot tolerate the environment they create. It can be said that organizations dissipate in the same way to rid themselves of bad management. But, an organization can also be understood as an equilibrium-seeking system that is extinguished when sufficient entropy accumulates, or a linear system that can be destroyed by uncontrolled disruption.

Most leadership scholars have always assumed that a *vision* or goal must be present first before the processes can be shaped toward the achievement of the goal. These scholars use the linear system as their level of inquiry, and they describe management in the classic sense. The *vision* advocated by most executives follows along the lines of increased profitability, and is either a refinement of convention or a correction of deviation but not a transformation. This vision may be a legitimate vision--that is, an image of the future--but it is the product of an individual, and may not be widely shared by others. For an explanation of what we experience of leadership as a collective process, it would be more instructive to take the position that the *vision* emerges out of the dynamics of the unfolding processes and not entirely from the mind of a single individual.

The *vision* beheld within a dissipative system is not as much chosen as it is recognized. Yet, that does not mean that this *vision* is entirely spontaneous. Transforming systems are *reciprocal*, they exchange energy with their environments. The *vision* of a leadership process is the result, in part, of a collective influence of the participants' wishes and consequent actions as part of the environmental forces. The leader's vision is only one element of those collective forces even though, as both Rost and Burns have suggested, it may provide more influence on the process than other elements. If the leader is skilled at statesmanship, then her or his vision could very well be garnered from the desires of the *polis*, and stated in such a way that the people recognize their ethics in the statement.

It is entirely possible for the leader to provide a substantial contribution to outcomes in a transforming system. When that happens, the leader's role in the system is to facilitate dissipation of old structures and transformation to new. The leader then represents deviation from convention. Deviation from convention is not the same as reformation of convention. A multitude of potential deviations from convention are available at any given moment in any given social milieu. Commonly, they are not recognized or acknowledged because people do not usually permit deviation to intrude upon their collective sensibilities except to condemn it. When convention becomes untenable, then group members open to deviations as potential solutions to their problems. A person who consistently holds an unconventional view may be considered a deviant right up until the time when that unconventional view is widely *discovered* by others as the way to go. The leader may be merely an advocate of a form of deviation that one day emerges as a representation of the desired transformation. A deviant may advocate a particular outcome or course of action for a long period of time, ignored by the *polis*, until suddenly conditions indicate to the general, shared consciousness that this course of action is the correct one. The leader is then viewed as *visionary* when it is the *polis* that has finally become visionary.

While management can be understood as an activity of building, leadership must be understood as a process of unfolding. Building has as its goal the creation of hierarchical structure from bottom to top--top to bottom. "Unfolding, in contrast, implies the interweaving of processes which lead simultaneously to phenomena of structuration at different hierarchical levels" (Jantsch, 1980, p. 75). What we experience as leadership is a process that organizes discontinuous cycles of energy exchanges that extend through the social milieu.

The Process of Leadership Defined

From a linear systems perspective, a process is understood as something that can be represented by a flow chart where decisions and tasks move from point to point in a linear fashion and in predictable ways. But, a social process is more like the emptiness of a bowl--while it is always there, it can only be defined by its container. In the case of leadership, the container is the cultural and political context within which the process exists. Schein (1992) correctly stressed that "neither culture nor leadership, when one examines each closely, can really be understood by itself" (p. 5).

The leadership process is like a river. It is a stream of energy, contained by its bed (the culture; the *polis*). Even though it can be said to be flowing in one direction, upon close examination parts of it flow sideways, in circles, or even backwards relative to the overall direction. It is constantly changing in speed and strength, and it constantly reshapes its own container. Under certain conditions, it is very unified in direction and very powerful; under other conditions it may be weak and languid. It may be shallow or deep, and it may flow in many directions at once.

Defining leadership as a social process is certainly not a new idea. Gemmill and Oakley (1992) defined leadership as "a process of dynamic collaboration, where individuals and organization members authorize themselves and others to interact in ways that experiment with new forms of intellectual and emotional meaning" (p. 124). This definition was offered as a remedy to the view of leadership based in the traits of the leader, which functions as a means for followers to avoid responsibility and initiative. Gemmill and Oakley used a framework of alienation and learned helplessness as a context for their discussion of leadership, and their definition allows for dissipation as a course for the process. The approach adopted by Gemmill and Oakley has considerable merit, and it can be further clarified by incorporating an understanding of the motives for collaboration and experimentation.

Without belaboring points made above, the key ideas may be summarized as the following: First, leadership is a process that is not specifically a function of the person in charge. Leadership is a function of the social system within which it occurs--a function of individual wills and of individual needs, and it is the result of the dynamics of collective will organized or mobilized to meet those various needs. Second, leadership is a process of adaptation and of evolution; it is a process of dynamic exchange and the interchanges of value. Leadership is deviation from convention, and is far from equilibrium. Third, leadership is a process of energy, not of structure. These ideas may help to establish a broad definition of leadership that indicates at a foundational level the nature of the process described by Gemmill and Oakley. Leadership, then, can be defined as *a process of transformative change where the ethics of individuals are integrated into the mores of a community as a means of evolutionary social development.*

Transformative change is structural change. While this form of change is possible and sometimes desirable in organizations, there are times and situations when it is disruptive and undesirable. If there is no need for change, then there is no need for leadership. Management is used to maintain stability within a linear system, and perfectly suited to that function. When there is a critical mass of individuals who feel change is needed, these individuals begin to realize that they can pursue their own needs by joining the collective movement. Then, they are motivated to adapt their self-interest to shared goals. The *leader* may symbolize that adaptation, but not normally be the source of it. When leadership occurs, it can take a form similar to the democratic processes that Plato and Aristotle shunned as disruptive to the social order.

Individuals may display conventional work behavior when motivated by a sense of duty to fulfill perceived obligations or when under the belief that such a display will lead to further reward. An individual's commitment to community goals and to structure can only emanate from the individual, not from the individual's organizational superior. The individual may be inspired by the boss, but no one works hard simply to make someone else rich.

If leadership is conceptualized as a *dynamic* process of interaction that creates change, then the leadership roles may not be, perhaps should not be, clearly defined. Gemmill and Oakley (1992) asserted that the presence of well-defined leaders may decrease the group's ability to experiment. This view of leadership greatly diminishes the importance (or relevance) of the leader's characteristics, abilities, and behaviors. If leadership is a democratic process, then no one person does an inordinate amount of leading, and every group member performs some leadership function at some point in time.

Joshua Lawrence Chamberlain--Civil War General, Hero of Gettysburg, Governor of Maine, and President of Bowdoin College-- reflected on what Abraham Lincoln meant to the men in the field. His thoughts were delivered in a speech to a large audience who had gathered at the Academy of Music in Philadelphia on Lincoln's birthday in 1909.

Chamberlain, who was himself a leader by so many definitions, characterized effectively the nature of leadership:

> Great crises in human affairs call out the great in men. But true greatness is not in nor of the single self; it is of that larger personality, that shared and sharing life with others, in which, each giving of his best for their betterment, we are greater than ourselves; and self surrender for the sake of that great belonging, is the true nobility (quoted in Wallace, 1995, p. 301).

Chapter 6

Leadership as a Relationship

A social process, as defined in the previous chapter, is much broader than a social relationship. A social relationship is based in a set of role expectations that are--theoretically, if not in practice--understood by the participants in the relationship. Relationships in our society tend to be contractual things, with performance standards and methods of evaluation. Social processes include social relationships, but they also provide for the development and definition of roles and role expectations where none may have existed, and they include ways that people have an effect upon each other apart from our usual ideas about relationships. Leadership relationships are based in role expectations, and are therefore contractual in nature. But the leadership process provides the vehicle for creating leadership relationships. For this reason, the leadership process must be understood before the leadership relationships and the leadership roles can be defined.

Defining The Undefinable

"The Tao that can be trodden is not the enduring and unchanging Tao. The name that can be named is not the enduring and unchanging name. (Conceived of as) having no name, it is the Originator of heaven and earth; (conceived of as) having a name, it is the Mother of all things" (Legge, 1962, p. 47).

These introductory lines from the *Tao Te Ching* imply, at an ontological level, that what we experience in the physical world is merely a manifestation of a source that lies beyond our ability to describe it accurately. In the beginning was the *word*; in the beginning was the *point*; in the beginning was the *source*. If the *source* is defined, the conceptual framework and the methods used to create the definition, as well as the definition itself, are all manifestations of the *source*. Trying to define the *source* is like trying to use a knife to cut itself. By way of example, Pirsig (1975) noted that, even though it makes an empirically verifiable difference in the world, *quality* cannot be defined directly. *Quality* can only be known through the qualities of things; *quality* is the source of the qualities that things possess. We can come to surprising levels of agreement about what has *quality*, but we cannot define it adequately without referring to those things in which quality is manifested.

Perhaps what makes leadership so hard to discuss is that we may *know* (conceive of) its source but not be able to describe it. What we can describe is but an interpretation of its manifestation in the world. The definition of leadership as a process presented in the last chapter is an attempt to establish an ontological standing for the source of the leadership we experience. That definition does not address the experience itself. The experience of leadership is an experience of a relationship. What we are able to define of the leadership experience is that which is manifested in *leadership relationships*. Having defined leadership as a process is only half of the journey--half of the definition. For an understanding of the process to be applicable, leadership must also be defined as a social relationship, and the leader's role relative to any other participants in that relationship must be considered. Only then may leadership education and practice be formulated and carried out.

The Conventional View Of The Leadership Relationship

The industrial paradigm of leadership frames its construct within a dyadic supervisor/subordinate relationship, such as that described by Yammarino (1995). This construct is founded in the feudal touchstone of citizenship: one's relationship with one's king. The industrial version of this relationship incorporates several assumptions held over from the feudal model: (a) that the king deserves allegiance by virtue of rank and/or of birthright, (b) that there is a natural, hierarchical difference in status, intelligence, and ability between the king and the subjects, and (c) that the subject's role, indeed obligation, is to serve the king's wishes.

Consequently, industrial leadership scholars tend to make the following assumptions: (a) that anyone who holds a supervisory position has been "anointed" by some process of selection, and is necessarily a leader who is appropriate for study as such, (b) that supervisors necessarily have abilities and traits that set them apart from subordinates and which led to their selection as leaders, and (c) that loyalty, worth, and moral behavior among subordinates is judged relative to measures of productivity, which are defined by the organizational objectives as articulated by supervisors. Leadership training, then, amounts to instruction in methods for manipulating the activities and exploiting the good will of subordinates (which is supervision), for bargaining and negotiating to achieve desired ends (which is statesmanship), and for developing and maintaining status differences and perceptions of status differences (which is command).

The feudal construct of leadership in the form of an inspirational or charismatic supervisory relationship characterizes subordinates as happy slaves who will work hard as the ultimate goal (perhaps it is a fantasy) of leadership just because their master is charismatic. There can be no denial that charisma has an effect on people, and that it contributes to outcomes. Charisma is a result of applied value, and it does, in many cases, explain a good deal of the apparent motivation to act. But, the leadership relationship must be understood as an outcome, or potential outcome, of the leadership process, and not simply as a direct result of the application of supervisory *style*. The leadership relationship is as much the result of charisma as the sum total of learning is the result of the application of one specific teaching method.

The Function of Leadership

As stated previously, the function of leadership as a social process is to facilitate collectively desired change, and some speculation on the need for change would be helpful for developing an understanding of leadership relationships. The vast literature describing thinking on the subject of social change cannot possibly be given adequate treatment here. However, there is a specific theory of the cycles of social change upon which much of the literature is indirectly based that may be instructive for building a context for the broader functions of leadership. That theory was advanced by Machiavelli in *the Discourses*.

Aristotle (1962) postulated that there are three forms of governments--monarchy, aristocracy, and democracy--and that these forms each have their negative manifestations--respectively tyranny, oligarchy, and anarchy. Machiavelli (1950) took that idea one step further by suggesting that, because of natural tendencies for established structures to decay, each of these six forms is one step in a multiphase cycle of structural growth and decline. The cycle progresses as follows.

Foremost, whatever form of government that is in place is more the result of chance than of design, even though its progression is marked by contrivance. People, living in a dangerous and often lethal world, desire to be unified for some measure of security, and choose the strongest and most courageous among them to lead. They place their trust in this leader, and grant their obedience and service in support of their common cause. Placing themselves thus on an equal footing with each other in support of their leader, they are in a position to witness the behavior of others and to distinguish good and honest from bad and vicious. Seeing those who bring harm to their benefactor (leader) arouses two sentiments: hatred for the offender, and love for the offended. The love for the offended is inspired not only by humanitarian impulses, but also by the realization that, without sanctions, anyone may be thus offended. The result is the creation of a set of laws used to promote a collective concept of justice. Also a result is the tendency, upon choosing the next monarch, to favor characteristics of wisdom and justice over strength and bravery.

While strength and bravery may be tested directly, wisdom and justice take time to evaluate. Assuming that children inherit characteristics of their parents, people use heredity as an indicator of character and institutionalize rules of succession. Born into obligation and privilege, the children inevitably choose the privilege over the obligation and degenerate from their parents' moral values. Self-indulgent and pleasure-seeking children of monarchs reject whatever feelings of responsibility their parents might have felt toward the governed, and pursue lives of waste and excess . The people quickly grow to hate and resent their new monarch, who responds defensively and becomes a tyrant.

When the tyrant's behavior becomes intolerable, certain courageous, selfless souls emerge from the masses to lead them in revolt. The grateful masses submit to these chiefs as their liberators, with the understanding that a new government will be formed that will replace the now despised monarchy with rule by this small, trusted group. Bearing the past tyranny in mind, this group of aristocrats will often govern in strict accordance with the new laws that they establish for themselves and will place public interest over their own.

The conscientious aristocrats are replaced by their children (successive generations) who have no memory of the events or circumstances that brought this form of government into being. The children quickly degenerate into self-indulgence and the aristocracy becomes an oligarchy. The people again rebel, this time structuring a popular government to replace the corruption of the elite few. Within a generation or two, people forget what circumstances necessitated the creation of this democratic government, and through neglect it degenerates into anarchy.

> Each individual only consulted his own passions, and a thousand acts of injustice were daily committed, so that constrained by necessity, or directed by the counsels of some good man, or for the purpose of escaping from this anarchy, they returned anew to the government of a prince, and from this they generally lapsed again into anarchy, step by step, in the same manner and from the same causes as we have indicated. (Machiavelli, 1950, p. 114)

The truth of this theory of social progress lies more in anecdotal recognition than in empirical research. But it does stress the continuity of good and bad in human nature. And, it does indicate points of change punctuated by circumstances often characterized as leadership. If the point of change is a successful revolution, then it is characterized as *good* leadership. If the circumstance is degeneration, it is characterized as *bad* leadership. We can now see that one may not exist without the other, and together they formulate the continuous nature of social organization and disorganization. This description of social development illustrates the dissipative character of social systems--continuous self-generation and dissipation--and the form predictability takes when applied to transformative systems.

The Leadership Relationship

Leadership is a particular form of social relationship. It cannot be understood as anything more tangible than as a temporal property of the actor (Foster, 1986). "Leadership is a transient phenomenon, one which can be practiced equally well by different social players, depending on the circumstances and the strength of ideas" (p. 3). Foster proposed three ideas for approaching the study of leadership:

First, leadership involves the demystification (penetration) of structure (social structure). Social structure is not a product of design as much as it is an outcome of the collective behavior and decision making of a multitude of individuals pursuing *eudaimonia*--the enjoyment and fulfillment one experiences when doing something presumed to be of *consequence*. If structure is not supporting *eudaimonia*, it will be changed; in order for it to be changed meaningfully, it must be understood. So, understanding the leadership relationship begins with knowledge of the nature and properties of social structures.

Second, leadership involves being politically critical and critically educative. The aim of education, as will be argued later in this chapter, is to understand the nature of the moral order and the role of conventional knowledge in its existence. The goal of learning is to more effectively solve problems. Critical thinking is the only viable route toward the objectification and the deconstruction of conventional knowledge. Political criticism is aimed at justice, and at improvements, or at least changes, to political relationships and to the policies for distributing power and resources defined or interpreted according to the constitution.

Third, leadership is conditioned on language. Language consists of cultural symbols for social structures, cultural mores, and shared cultural values. So, language is a key component of the content of leadership. The praxis of leadership, according to Foster, is transformative action: "the ability of all persons to engage in acts of leadership which help in the transformation to a way of life which incorporates participative principles" (p. 18). Leadership is, in a word, citizenship, and it is the result of the actions of many rather than of one individual.

Foster demonstrated that leadership is a political relationship that has critical assessment at its root. According to Burns (1978), the common good emerges from chaotic, reciprocal interaction among people with potentially conflicting goals, values, and ideals. This interaction includes mutual influencing, bargaining, coalition building, behavior guided by parochial attitudes, conflict over scarce resources, and competition for control. Even though there may be a set of rules used to facilitate the process, it is not a controlled or a rational process. Rational problem solving approaches have little if any real effect by this view of leadership because, if for no other reason, knowledge itself is a formulation of incomplete data, of parochial perceptions, of partisan analysis, and of socially constructed reality.

An evolutionary attempt by Joseph Rost (1991) to define leadership as a nonsupervisory relationship reflects the idea that leadership is based in complex interaction. Rost, building upon ideas expressed by Burns, defined leadership as "an influence relationship among leaders and their collaborators who intend real changes that reflect their mutual purposes" (Rost, 1993, p. 99). Rost made the point carefully that there are no *followers* in this relationship because everyone is involved in the same relationship, hence the word collaborators.

Rost's definition is augmented by four essential elements:

(1) The relationship is based in multidirectional influence. The *leader* is equally subject to changing attitudes, motives, and directions with everyone else.

(2) Multiple actors are active in the relationship, there typically is more than one leader, and the influence is inherently unequal. The *leader* is not the only source of the outcomes, and may potentially be the most or the least contributor.

(3) Leaders and their collaborators intend, but do not necessarily produce, real changes in the future. While supervision is measured strictly by results, leadership is measured by intent rather than by results.

(4) Leaders and their collaborators have mutual or common purposes that reflect their intended changes. The purpose of the group and the changes intended by the group are not dictated by an individual or by an outside source. They are the product of a collaborative effort.

Rost's definition can be summarized in the following way: Leadership is a dynamic social and political relationship that is based in a mutual development of purposes which may never be realized. The concept of leadership as a non-supervisory relationship is characterized by the words *dynamic* and *mutual*, ideas suggested by Burns.

James MacGregor Burns offered the following criticism of Rost's construct in his Foreword to Rost's book: "I suggest that despite his intense and impressive concern about the role of values, ethics, and morality in transforming leadership, he underestimates the crucial importance of these variables. Even more I miss. . . a grasp of the role of great conflict in great leadership" (Rost, 1991, p. xii). Although Burns praised Rost's work as "one of the indispensable works on leadership," he felt that Rost leaned toward "consensus procedures and goals that I believe erode such leadership" (p. xii). Then added "but Rost's main theme towers over such criticism" (p. xii).

What Burns did not find in Rost's work was a clarification of the sort of conflict to be found in leadership when one takes a dissipative view of that process. Nor did he perceive Rost's construct to support the sort of moral transformation one would expect to find as a result of chaotic redefinition of social and personal identity. Specifically, what Burns did not find was a focus on the leader as the supervisor of conflict and governor of transformation. Burns, in his own work, seemed to have held on to the view of the leader as a statesman, wielding power and influence, fighting for a greater good. Burns did not seem to appreciate

Rost's clear attempt to leave the heroic, forceful, trait-ridden leader out of it.

Rost was attempting to define leadership in a cross-cultural way as an influence relationship within which the leader's role as a supervisor, as a commander, and as a statesman is minimized as a source of outcomes. The consensus building that Burns assumed to be undermining the supervisory capacity of the leader is in fact Rost's recognition that the leadership role passes from person to person, and that the person in charge is rarely, if ever, in control of the process.

Leadership can be understood as a relationship through Rost's (1991) four essential elements. The first of these elements states that the leadership relationship is based in multidirectional influence. This statement is a simple way of characterizing the complexity of a transforming system in which the outcomes are not always the result of standardized procedures, such as the application of organizing structure. Without necessarily having stated it directly, Rost implied that multidirectional influence can be expected to produce conflict, and that coercion used to minimize conflict would be a part of another sort of relationship. If there is not direct competition for the *leader's position*, there is certainly competition to promote personal values and priorities. In part, Burns' objection to this element of Rost's definition might have been answered by a statement of recognition that all forms of social interaction can be expected to contain some coercion or attempts at coercion.

Rost maintained that the influence behaviors that people in the relationship employ are noncoercive, even though they rely upon *power resources*. Power resources are made up of reputation, prestige, personality, perceived intelligence, and so forth that make one person seem different from other persons. Power resources are used to persuade. Rost was careful to differentiate power resources from authority, because leadership is not based in authority relationships. Authority is a contractual relationship that has a priori expectations for certain outcomes in both directions. Supervision is a relationship founded in authority and responsibility. Authority is based in the power to reward and to punish and not in the power to persuade, and therefore response to authority is based in fear--fear of death, fear of failure, fear of losing status or wealth, etc.

The second element of Rost's definition states that there are no *followers* in the leadership relationship. Multiple actors are active in the relationship, and there typically is more than one leader. This element is a recognition that the *leader* is not the only source of the outcomes. Outcomes in a transforming system are the result of a complex exchange of energy among its elements and with the environment.

A leadership process occurring in a social group or organization is not self-contained or isolated from the environment. While conscious influences and activities take place within a given group and within a given context--office, church, meeting hall, etc.--participants are exposed to many other forms of influence not physically present in group gatherings. Participants can be influenced by what they have seen on television, by conversations they had in the laundromat, by heated exchanges with a relative, by being stuck in traffic, by noticing age spots on their hands, or by a host of other potential sources. These influences are brought to bear on the dynamic problem solving activities conducted by participants in the process.

For example, a man has an argument with his wife. He storms out of his house, roars off in his car, and cuts off a plumber on the freeway. The annoyed plumber dwells on this slight while working on an architect's home plumbing and forgets to tighten a valve. The architect's wife comes home to discover two inches of water on the floor, and calls her husband. The husband is angry and distracted and becomes abrupt to a female coworker. The coworker is involved in an activist group that is putting together a petition for revisions in policy to the school board. By the next meeting of this group, she has decided that civility and fairness are her top priorities, and argues persuasively for a new paragraph in the petition. She never met the couple who argued, but they have influenced her behavior and consequently the process of leadership. This is a simple example of the potential for complexity in a transforming social system, and the reason that the leader may potentially be the least contributor to the outcomes.

Rost's third element states that leaders and their collaborators intend, but do not necessarily produce, real changes. Leadership is a process of dynamic exchange of energy. While the process always produces outcomes, it may not necessarily produce desired or intended outcomes. The industrial model of leadership uses feudal expectations for monarchs as standards by which the outcomes of leadership are measured. If leaders are thought to be the source of leadership, then it follows that they are responsible for outcomes and that outcomes should be determined and implemented by rational methods.

If leadership is understood as a transformative process, then outcomes, while not necessarily arbitrary, are less predictable and less likely to be the result of specific intention. Transforming systems cannot be limited to specific influences, nor can they be understood by isolating specific influences for study. They draw upon influences that are often ignored, overlooked, or misunderstood by observers. Results may be understood through post hoc analysis, but are predictable only to the extent that the observer has some degree of *clinical experience* with the process. The process of leadership can only be measured by intent, and not by results. Measuring performance to goals is the control function of management, and characterizes the sort of supervisory relationship that is appropriately applied in a classic system.

Rost's fourth element states that leaders and their collaborators have mutual or common purposes that reflect their intended changes. Intentions are based in values. Values are experienced in different ways by different people and at different times. The coworker described above had an experience that energized her will to act relative to particular values that guided her actions and motivated her to act on those values. Her values were not created by the experience, but brought to bear on the specific problems to be solved. This is an example of the "common and infinitesimally small elements by which the masses are moved" to which Tolstoy was referring.

Experience shapes action to the extent that it rearranges perceptions of priorities and the conditions under which action is taken. What we see is not necessarily the classic action/reaction--the coworker did not direct her action toward the architect, but toward another goal. It is possible that she was not consciously aware of the source of her motivation to act. Her purpose in acting was not necessarily inspired by group processes, but became an integral part of the group's common purpose because members of this group probably shared similar values. The purpose of the group--*our telos*--and the changes the group intends to make are the result of complex interaction of experience and value. The group's purpose is not dictated by an individual, nor by any single outside source.

The definition of leadership as a relationship must be taken as a qualified expansion of the understanding of leadership as a process. The leadership process manifests itself in relationships among human beings, most of whom will never completely grasp the nature and sources of the process in which they are involved, even though they have similar experiences of it. Compiling Rost's ideas into a single statement, we may say that leadership is *a dynamic social and political relationship that is based in complex social interaction, collective grasp and realization of shared individual values, and a mutual development of purposes which may never be realized.* This relationship is nonsupervisory, nonlinear, dissipative, and potentially influenced by an infinite number of unidentifiable sources. This relationship can occur within a context of management, from which plans, structure, direction, and control may be used to guide the conduct of the relationship.

The Role of the Leader

Taking the process approach to an understanding of leadership is not easy for those who are enculturated in the industrial paradigm. Burns (1978) had a difficult time articulating his ideas about social processes using industrial language. For example, in his discussion of revolutionary leadership (Chapter 8) he recognized that the *leaders* of the French Revolution were mediators between popular *subleaders* (read "symbols of value") and the masses. Yet, he could not excuse himself from the industrial obligation to discuss leadership in terms of traits that can be applied to kings or CEOs: "What can be said broadly of revolutionary leadership? It is passionate, dedicated, single-minded, ruthless, self-assured, courageous, tireless, usually humorless, often cruel" (p. 239). These traits, of course, can be found in people of any given situation or consequence, and Burns opened himself to his own criticism of focusing more on the leader than on leadership.

The compulsion to address traits arises from an oversimplification of the role of the leader. In his discussion of group leadership, Burns cited Freud's observation that when groups lose their leaders, there is often panic and disarray. Further, he cited Whyte's study of street gangs as an example of the critical role of the central leader in maintaining cohesion in the group. But this is a view strictly of the *supervisory* role of the leader. It is this view that demands discussion of traits and style. It is this view that channels any understanding of leadership into theories of supervision. Overly simplifying the role of the leader as a supervisor is a natural outcome of the obligation to justify the exploitation of work behavior in an industrial economy. This obligation relative to the supervisory role of the leader has effectively discouraged any other view that might distinguish leadership from supervision.

Leadership and supervision are different forms of social organization that contain subtle but profound differences in their respective fabrics of social relationships, and, consequently, in social outcomes. Ostensively, it is difficult to separate the two concepts because leadership can occur within a context of supervision. To use a quick example of the difference, consider a combat unit. When the unit *leader* is killed during a battle, the potential demoralization and chaos that can and frequently does follow is an oft cited example of the critical nature of leadership. However, when disorder does follow, what was present initially was a supervisory relationship and not a leadership relationship.

If leadership by the process definition was present, there would be little if any noticeable disruption--beyond natural grieving for a fallen comrade and loss of an able body--and the supervisory role would be quickly assumed by another group member. Why? Because a community fabric of relationships would have established a collective understanding of the group's mission and each member's respective role. Members of the unit know their roles relative to their *telos*, and can act their roles without the supervisory direction that had been provided by the original commander. In other words, when leadership is present and working as a process of integration, profound supervision is unneeded because everyone knows who *we* are, where *we* are going, and how *we* expect to get there. The loss of the symbol of what *we* all want merely allows for another symbol to emerge, because what *we* all want has not changed. It is possible for the person who symbolized *our telos* to die, and for that symbol to remain present in our minds in the manner of saints and prophets.

Since the literature on industrial leadership addresses primarily theories of supervision, there is little that can or should be rehearsed on that subject in a discussion of post-industrial leadership. Virtually all aspects of extracting performance and directing the activities of others have been explored and discussed by industrial leadership scholars. Therefore, the leadership relationship will be discussed here with as little reference as possible to supervision. It will not be easy for that goal to be accomplished because the two ideas have been so closely associated for so long.

One important role for the leader is that of facilitator. Facilitation in the sense meant here is characterized by skills in statesmanship, which are more complex skills than those normally implied by the words *coaching, mediating,* and *inspiring.* Statesmanship implies mobilization and careful manipulation of dynamic elements of a continuous whole toward some end. Statesmanship includes skills in coaching, mediating, influencing, bargaining, coalition building, etc., but does not in itself characterize the comprehensive and reciprocal nature of the leadership relationship. Statesmanship pertains only to what is potentially a leader's role in the relationship. Given that there may be multiple leaders, many individuals with such skills may be working together, or they may be working against each other.

For Burns, as noted above, distinguishing leadership from other social forms of organization was difficult. In the first place, Burns was obsessed with the psychoanalyses of great leaders, and seemed to imply that this form of character analysis can explain the bulk of the nature of leadership. He noted that leaders are seekers of power, and that they desire to gain total control of everything around them in order to carry out their intentions. He did not address the possibilities for reluctant or for unambitious leaders. His orientation is understandable given that he is a student of political science. He noted that power differentials exist in a relationship whether or not they are sought, and that this power is a function of the context and motivations of the power recipients. He also noted that these power relationships can have a transforming effect on all those involved--which he called *transforming leadership*.

Key to the discussion of power relationships is the concept of causation--the leader causes the follower to do X to Z. In a discussion of causation, the distinction among the concepts of leadership, supervision, statesmanship, and coercion becomes blurred. Given that outcomes of each of these concepts have causes, they must necessarily be different causes. If they all had the same causes, then there would be no need to have so many words to describe the same thing. Most discussions of causation focus on the *leader*. The result of assuming the *leader* as causal is a treatment of leadership, supervision, statesmanship, and coercion all as the same thing to a different degree.

Supervision depends upon a socially defined and conventional source for authority. In Daniel Defoe's *Robinson Crusoe*, the title character did not hesitate to assume a superior, supervisory social standing over Friday based upon his *civilized* nature and *good breeding* even though Friday appeared in many ways to be his physical and mental superior. Indeed, not only did Crusoe feel justified in assuming authority, he presumed to change Friday's name and identity to suit his own needs--I do not understand your language, therefore I will call you what I please and you will learn my language and religion; your truth is incorrect, so you will learn mine. We are led to believe that Friday happily abandoned his culture and the moral order he previously lived every day of his life to embrace this new subordinate role and new identity. Friday was portrayed as eager to have his loyalty as a servant tested at every turn. He was the ideal subordinate. That would not be the outcome had I written the story.

On the other hand, I would not have become known as a great author.

This is one form of socially recognized power to which Burns was referring. Yet the ardent zeal of some to supervise and of others to be supervised does not provide a sound footing for an understanding of the social fabric of leadership, particularly when leadership is understood as that punctuation of change between states of social organization. The concept of supervision minimizes the role of conflict and experimentation in social development; supervision limits development to that which is defined by the supervisor.

In addition to supervision, Burns implied that statesmanship is the power ability needed by leaders. Statesmanship depends upon socially defined protocol and methods for negotiating. Statesmanship, a concept which captures many of the *leadership skills* often alluded to in discussions of industrial leadership, is the ability to bargain and to negotiate, to perceive and to sway public opinion, to frame the face of the issue, to understand and to work within the rules of the game, to mobilize support and to build coalitions, and to use propaganda, partisan analysis, and disinformation effectively to accomplish ends. Statesmanship is the skill needed for social control when direct supervision is not effective or appropriate. Many times when great national or international figures are acknowledged for their great leadership, it is their statesmanship that merits the attention. But, leadership and statesmanship are not the same thing. The two different words represent differently experienced phenomena. Statesmanship is experienced as the skill an individual has, and leadership is experienced as a relationship among a group of individuals.

Leadership depends upon social definitions as well as supervision or statesmanship do. Supervision depends upon a socially defined authoritarian structure that organizes work and regulates conflict; statesmanship depends upon a socially defined protocol that structures competitive interaction; leadership depends upon a common understanding of a *telos* that provides social direction. Because an understanding of *telos* is not necessarily universal within a given group, there will always be conflict associated with elements of the moral order over and above personality differences between individuals.

First, unless the group is blessed with abundance there will be conflict over the distribution of scarce resources that are needed to satisfy basic human wants and needs. Much of this first sort of conflict can be created by a power structure that allows some individuals to withhold resources as profit or as instruments of reward and punishment that can be used to increase their power. Conflict over basics is less prevalent when *our telos* demands that everyone share equally, even if we all must do without.

Second, there will be conflict over the use of resources relative to environmental conditions--that is, those resources that are used to satisfy created needs. The rarity of gold is relative, and no one cares about gold unless it has a socially defined value. Environments where gold is very abundant or nonexistent will not encourage conflict over gold. People do not need air conditioning unless they believe they do.

Third, there will be conflict over what constitutes a social problem and how it should be solved. These conflicts establish social priorities and can become institutionalized. "The question, then, is not the inevitability of conflict but the function of leadership in expressing, shaping, and curbing it" (Burns, 1978, pp. 37-38).

According to Burns, conflict is intrinsically compelling. Even though Burns focused upon great individuals as managers or facilitators of conflict, he recognized the role of conflict in the process of social development: "It is leadership that draws the crowd into the incident, that changes the number of participants, that closely affects the manner of the spread of the conflict, that constitutes the main 'processes' of relating the wider public to the conflict" (p. 38). In other words, it is leadership that encourages and reinforces choices of association, the parameters of association, the structure of social relationships, and the commitment to *our telos*. The role of conflict in leadership is to force individuals to clarify to themselves and to others their own values and priorities, and to seek other individuals who will support what has been clarified.

Rost (1991) distinguished leadership from management (read "supervision") by stating that the former is based in influence while the latter is based in authority. Many authors suggest that the leadership relationship, whether it is influence or authority, is based in power. There is only one true form of power--the power over fear. No one has any real power over a person who is not afraid. It could be argued that having a person killed is power over life and death. But real power over life is the ability to create life. The real power over death is the ability to abstain from dying. Many people are afraid of dying, of failing, of losing their jobs, or of being poor, and these fears make them more susceptible to supervision. The skillful manipulation of those fears has for the past century passed as one of the characteristics of successful leadership--that which Rost identified as authority.

If we say that *authority* is based in fear, we then must differentiate *influence* by saying that it is connected with hope and with faith. Hope and faith are what drive away fear. To make sense of a relationship that is a manifestation of the process of people collectively seeking *eudaimonia*, we must adopt faith and hope as the *substance* of the leadership relationship. That is not to say that people in that relationship do not have fears, or that at least some of their motivation to become involved in that relationship is inspired by fear. It is to say that the relationship is founded in the hope for a better world (as defined by the group) and faith that effort expended in this collective action will bring about some measure of improvement.

Training Leaders

Training is aimed at improving skills. The sort of skills considered valuable in an industrial society are technical skills, and include things like math, science, and problem solving. When an industrial society is casting about the globe searching for someone to teach it the technical skills that will help it to solve industrial problems, the net rarely hauls in anything from non-industrialized societies. So-called *eurocentric* education is focused on industrial parts of the world for a reason--that is, those are the people who have something to teach us about living in an industrial society. The sort of training carried out is directly related to the sort of problems that must be solved. Problem solving is successful or unsuccessful depending on two things: the methods used, and the way the problem is understood. Training is aimed at developing the methods, and education is aimed at understanding the problems.

Leadership training that emphasizes a set of definable and learnable skills and abilities can only be defended if leadership and management are defined in the same way. This is the view of leadership as excellent management or as a function of management. It is this view of leadership Rost (1991) criticized as overly rationalistic, goal-oriented, utilitarian, and materialistic in character, and that Gemmill and Oakley (1992) have convincingly debunked as a social myth, the function of which is to preserve existing organizational and social structures by shifting the responsibility for change to messiahs when no change is actually intended by those in power.

If leadership training does not focus upon technical skills and abilities, what should it focus upon? Klenke (1993) illustrated the conflict between the humanities disciplinary view of leadership that does not base arguments on collected data and the social science view that does. This conflict reduces clarity between what can be called management development and leadership education, or between being a doer and being a thinker. Klenke recommended solving this issue by avoiding the bipolar, dualistic thinking created by academic parochial perceptions, by giving the student "the freedom to pursue the ambiguities and paradoxes inherent in the study of leadership as an art and a science" (p. 119). This suggestion can be accomplished by emphasizing context, and by learning about leadership as a process.

Klenke suggested that leaders are developed through increased understanding of the moral obligations of leadership and acceptance of the responsibilities to serve one's community and society. Wren (1994) acknowledged the role of citizenship as a function of leadership by asserting that leadership education is increasingly important to this country "to produce citizens capable of confronting and resolving the complex problems which will face tomorrow's society" (p. 74). Wren felt strongly that the study of leadership should be based in the multi-disciplinary approach of the liberal arts.

The focus upon citizenship is derived from the past, particularly from Plato and Aristotle. Leadership as a collective activity was an essential element of Athenian democracy. While Plato was in favor of a class system form of society, he still associated what we experience as leadership with social development. Tucker (1981) characterized Plato's view of leadership as "an activity with utility for the polis, the activity of giving direction to the community of citizens in the management of their common affairs, especially with a view to the training and improvement of their souls" (p. 3). The reference to improvement of the soul, a common theme in Plato's works, is the historic link of leadership and ethics (or virtue); it is what Burns referred to as something that "engages the full person" (1978, p. 4).

The view of organizations as political communities can answer a number of perplexing questions about the moral component of leadership and the way in which leaders are prepared. People seek organizations that provide them with a sense of *polis*, and commit themselves to political citizenship to the extent that they feel attached to the community. Leadership is democratic, and democracy relies upon a cultural orientation toward *citizenship* for its existence. Leadership education, then, must focus upon that which facilitates the understanding of one's citizenship responsibility:

(1) existing organizational or social structures and systems and how they have developed,

(2) the metaphysical assumptions that individuals hold regarding the purpose of life, the nature of the world, and human nature that both unite us as communities and divide us as individuals,

(3) the values inherent in the prevailing moral order,

(4) how those values have developed,

(5) the implications of those values for choices of action,

(6) the' ways in which we can reflect upon our similarities and differences and order our wants and needs to produce change,

(7) analysis of cultural symbols that perpetuate and communicate the moral order,

(8) the process of cultural and moral transformation,

(9) the nature of political conflict over scarce resources and ideology,

(10) the manner in which policy is made,

(11) the various frames used to understand social problems and how these frames lead to various approaches to solutions, and

(12) the citizen's role in social and organizational development.

Where the feudal paradigm conceived of citizenship as subjugation and loyalty to the king, the emerging paradigm adopts a perspective of citizenship more akin to Athenian democracy. Leadership education, therefore, must be centered upon the role of all leadership participants as active shapers of their world, and not upon the role of leaders as social elites. The questions of life addressed through art and literature, the cycles of successes and failures of human endeavors explored by history, the institutions developed by social groups as understood by anthropology and sociology, the discipline and abstraction of mathematics, the analytical methods of philosophy, the exchange of ideas facilitated through rhetoric, and the influence of cognition, perception, and interaction defined by psychology all provide the bricks and mortar for building an appropriate construct of leadership for preparing the citizen to participate. The foundation must be metaphysical, broad in ontology and in method.

The modern liberal disciplines are infused with three essential problems that potentially interfere with the development of that foundation. First, empiricism and *experimenta lucifera* have replaced critical thinking and comprehensive understanding as a basis for education in social processes (Harré, et al., 1985; Hutchins, 1936). Scientism has imposed a reductionistic tendency to categorize and to analyze things to the point of meaninglessness. In addition, scientism imposes the need for discipline related jargon that hinders, if not prevents, communication among the disciplines and integration of their constructs. Scientism also promotes the a priori assumption of cause-effect relationships when they are not necessarily the best approach to explanation. The need to rationalize has clearly overwhelmed the need to interpret and to understand.

The second problem with liberal studies throughout the 20th Century was the tendency for colleges and universities to view their curricula as professional training (Hutchins, 1936). When faced with the expectations of students, their parents, employers, and society in general, teachers feel pressure to make liberal studies *relative*. That is, they focus upon tricks of the trade, or upon specific knowledge one might need as an employee. Under this condition, an advance in the field of study is often evaluated relative to its utility or application to productivity.

The third, and potentially worst problem, is that many academic disciplines may be built upon a fragmented, discontinuous, and misinterpreted set of theoretical propositions (MacIntyre, 1984). MacIntyre has suggested that philosophically based disciplines are founded in fragments of a conceptual scheme consisting of bits and pieces of language and theory that survived the censorship and intellectual restructuring conducted by the Christian Church in the Middle Ages. The revival of these studies during the Enlightenment pulled the fragments of knowledge and language together into a set of practices that has no coherency.

Although liberal studies can provide a framework for leadership studies, as disciplines in and of themselves they may not provide the support needed for exploring the relationships between socially constructed reality and social processes. Perhaps what is needed is a model of education that is consistent with the emerging paradigm of leadership. Relative to the three tier model of social psychology developed by Harré, et al. (1985) that was presented in Chapter Two, the totality of education can be allocated to three integrated components: training, development, and education.

The first tier of subconscious subroutines is clearly enhanced through training. For example, hitting a golf ball is a subroutine. Although the activity begins with conscious and deliberate movements, through training (and practice) it becomes more effective as it becomes a subconscious motion initiated by a conscious switch. Skills training is an activity that converts a capability to an ability through the structuring and practice of a set of behaviors. Training is used to create and reinforce the subroutines of behavior that are the substance of the lowest tier of the three tier system. Training can be specialized to enhance any specific ability and develop skill to the extent that the target activity becomes a subconscious subroutine.

For the view of leadership as a process, the only training worthwhile would focus upon those behaviors needed to *manage* the outputs of the process: namely, the changed or developed social structures, roles, and role expectations. A leadership process as defined above cannot be managed. Training could also possibly be used to help organize the potential of the inherent conflict among the participants in the process by developing political skills such as communicating, coalition building, compromising, and negotiating--in other words, training in statesmanship.

The second tier is enhanced through development of conscious control. Development is a process of self-analysis and is aimed at the integration of the intellectual and the emotional capabilities of an individual which result in self-motivation, self-direction, and self-identity. The purpose of development is to increase self-efficacy by providing students with both an understanding of themselves and a conventional base from which to explore new or conflicting ideas or experiences--in other words, they learn to *manage* themselves. Development is focused upon the conscious control of behavior, and hopefully enhances one's ability to create and to shape the basic skill subroutines.

Leadership development would require the exploration and development of personal values as they are reflections of the values of others that will be needed to facilitate participation in the process. Development should have as its goal the self-control needed for the individual to adapt and to integrate personal wants and needs with those of the group.

Education relative to the third tier, then, is a cognitive integration of conceptual knowledge, ideals, insight, and experiences that bring into awareness the social and cultural processes that affect one's own behavior. Assuming that all behavior is guided to a large extent by socially constructed reality, social values and by conventional morality, and that much of the influence of social context is beyond immediate awareness, the aim of education is to bring these influences into awareness and to explore the great varieties of behavioral responses possible under varying social conditions. The purpose of education is "to connect man with man, to connect the present with the past, and to advance the thinking of the race" (Hutchins, 1936, p. 71)--to create the basis from which collective decisions are made about the future. Education provides the foundations from which conventional knowledge, created by collective processes, may be deconstructed, examined, and reconstructed.

Education is that which facilitates a broad perspective or awareness of the human condition: the place and purpose of humans in the universe and their relationships with other entities. Development is that which produces a sense of identity, a sense of place in the society, a sense of control, and self-discipline. Training is that which imparts a skill or set of skills to be used in the act of living and working. Training is necessary for human productivity and enterprise. Development is necessary for the creation, organization, and maintenance of society. Education is necessary for human growth and self-actualization. Training provides for physical well-being; development provides for social well-being; education provides for spiritual well-being.

Training and developing managers requires a specific content. Managerial training may focus upon the skills needed to solve problems, to motivate people, and to manage organizations to accomplish goals. The aim of this type of training is to give managers ready tools to be used to minimize uncertainty and to avoid blame for uncontrollable outcomes. This form of training can be highly rational, formula oriented, and mechanistic.

Executive or managerial development must focus upon the personal traits and characteristics needed to cope with the demands of the managerial role. The aim of development is to prepare the manager physically and mentally for organizational politics, for unreasonable expectations, for incompatible coworkers and subordinates, for conflicting requirements for action, and for the slings and arrows of outrageous fortune. Development is somewhat less rationally oriented than training. It requires reflective insight and interpretation as well as the development of specific personal characteristics. Development can be based upon examination of complex sets of cause-effect relationships and their integration with specific skills.

Leadership education must be divorced from expectations of pragmatic application, even though it will eventually be applied. Education must view rational methods and cause-effect relationships as partial truth from which broader understanding and integration may proceed. The aim of leadership education is to bring basic assumptions, assimilated values, and predominant behavioral patterns into conscious awareness, and to understand their influences on decision making and human behavior. Education must be understood as more comprehensive and less goal-oriented than training or development. Leadership education is little more or less than self-awareness in the Socratic tradition, where analysis of cause-effect relationships gives way to the contemplation of the integration and synthesis of non-linear phenomena.

A Final Thought

Though he had something else in mind, Bass (1990) correctly pointed out that leadership does make a difference. Leadership can be directly experienced even if the possibility for direct observation of it is less certain. While few leadership scholars can agree on a definition, all can agree that some phenomenon we call *leadership* is present in the world. Leadership may be granted ontological standing by virtue of an Hegelian dialectic: Leadership is not supervision; leadership is not command; leadership is not management; leadership is not statesmanship.

It should be clear that the process view of leadership will make little sense to someone who *knows* that leadership is all about supervision or command--that is, the ability of the leader to get people to do what the leader wants them to do. The appeal of the simplicity and the comfort of equating leadership with the abilities and characteristics of the leader are enough for some people to reject any more complex notion. To many, this is merely a semantic issue; they *know* the sun circles the earth, every observation verifies it, and they see no point in arguing over words used to describe it. To others, this approach threatens a lifetime of building a career on a particular idea.

People can live in a many splendered bliss believing that the sun circles the earth, or believing that the leader is the source of leadership. But their adherence to this perception will not help them if they wish to explore outer space, or if they are spending their time, energy, and resources attempting to improve *leadership*.

In short, the process approach denies many well-established social institutions. It removes responsibility for outcomes almost completely from the leader and places it upon the group. It does not justify the blame commonly placed upon leaders for failure. It does not justify high executive salaries and perks. It does not justify our expectations for elected officials, nor our general apathy toward our individual roles in government and in social outcomes. It does not justify most scholarly activity currently conducted in the name of *leadership*. And, it does not support traditional approaches to leadership training.

Accepting the new paradigm does not necessarily require discarding the old. The industrial paradigm is a model of "one man command and control," and there are many problems for which the old paradigm may be an appropriate application: military campaigns, business competition, and orchestral conducting. The industrial paradigm functions more effectively if it is understood as management. That labeling removes much of the glory for executives and for leadership scholars alike, but some modern problems will need a new frame for definition, and solutions that are more effective than the current approaches.

Leadership theory and other theories of complex processes, such as the theory of evolution, may have explanatory value, but offer little in the way of predictive value. If we limit ourselves to rational or scientific approaches to understanding leadership that presume predictive power through knowledge of cause-effect relationships, then we will exclude much of the experience of leadership. People tend to experience leadership as exhilarating and inspirational (Burns, 1978). Although we commonly assume that experience is created by the leader, under different conditions that same leader may not be able to recreate that same experience. Our response to that failure has been to look to the situational variables, which we never seem to be able to pin down. Despite occasional statistically significant results, empirical methods rarely account for enough variance to make them predictive. Desiring control and having control are two different things. There is clearly a need to conceptualize leadership in a different way, and come to a more common understanding of what it is, if for no other reason than to cope with it.

It should be clear that empirical verification of the proposed definitions will not be easy, if it is in fact possible. Parry (1998) made a good case for using grounded theory as a method of researching the process of leadership. Does leadership evolve as a consequence of the environment responding to its demands, or as a creator of the environment? Or, both? What is the social purpose of leadership, and how is it entwined with the purpose of life and with the adult search for meaning? Social science research often assumes purpose or goals without actually attempting to define them because they are not observable. The assessment of progress is necessarily a matter of value.

The emerging paradigm of leadership requires us to reexamine, to redefine, and to reinstall the meaning of citizenship as a foundation of leadership. We must move quickly and decisively away from the glorification of the "one who stands alone" defying the system, shunning cooperation, and doing whatever it takes to win. Values must be deemphasized that have encouraged exploitation of people for the sake of making profits, and values must be reemphasized that help us to live well through cooperative efforts. So, too, we must begin to understand organizations not merely as capitalistic tools, but as communities that compete successfully for legitimacy by improving the human condition.

We all benefit when the community benefits. In spite of Emerson's (1983) admonition to be self-reliant, an individual's power is increased by the strength of the community much more than it is decreased by bureaucratic structures. An individual benefits much more through community improvement than by winning isolated competitions. There is little real value in being voted Most Valuable Player when you are on a team that finished last in the standings because its players did not form a *team*. We should not be looking to isolate an MVP; we should not care about the standings. A community is defined by the strength of its values, and by its commitment to their application. Creation of a sense of community requires more than a few simple activities. There must be ethical or spiritual dimensions, occupational dimensions, and dimensions of social and emotional support. Philosopher Julian Huxley felt that life is a struggle against frustration, ignorance, and suffering, but it is also a struggle for something of value (Gale, 1969).

A new view of science, of business, of politics, and ultimately of life must be adopted in conjunction with the definitions proposed here. A great deal more thought must be devoted to the epistemological issues and to consequences of the forms of measurement applied to social processes and the paradigms for problem solving they create: "I'm whatever your questions turn me into. Don't you see that? It's your questions that make me who I am" (Pirsig, 1991, p. 220).

References

Aristotle. (1969). *Nicomachean ethics* (D. Ross, Trans.). London: Oxford University Press.

Aristotle. (1962). *The politics* (Translated by T. A. Sinclair). Baltimore, MD: Penguin.

Aquinas, T. (1952). Summa theologica (Fathers of the English Dominican Province, Trans.). In R.M. Hutchins (Ed.). *Great books of the Western World.* Chicago: Encyclopedia Britannica.

Barker, R. A. (1994) Relative utility of culture and climate analysis to an organizational change agent: An analysis of General Dynamics/Electronics Division. *The International Journal of Organizational Analysis, 2,* 67-86.

Barker, R. A. (1993). An evaluation of the Ethics Program at General Dynamics. *Journal of Business Ethics, 12,* 165-77.

Bass, B. M. (1990). *Bass & Stogdill's handbook of leadership* (3rd ed.) New York: The Free Press.

Bass, B. M. (1981). *Stogdill's handbook of leadership* (rev. ed.). New York: The Free Press.

Bassiry, G. R., & Dekmejian, R. H. (1993, January-February). America's global companies: A leadership profile. *Business Horizons,* pp. 47-53.

Bauman, Z. (1994). Morality without ethics. *Theory, Culture & Society, 11,* 1-34.

Benedict, R. (1934). *Patterns of culture.* Boston: Houghton Mifflin.

Bennis, W. G. (1959). Leadership theory and administrative behavior: The problem with authority. *Administrative Science Quarterly, 4,* 259-301.

Bennis, W. G. & Nanus, B. (1985). *Leaders: The strategies for taking charge.* New York: Harper & Row.

Bidney, D. (1953). *Theoretical anthropology.* New York: Columbia University Press.

Bloom, A. (1987). *The closing of the American mind.* New York: Simon & Schuster.

Boyce, M. (1979). *Zoroastrians: Their religious beliefs and practices.* London: Routledge & Kegan Paul.

Bohannan, P. (1963). *Social anthropology.* New York: Holt, Rinehart & Winston.

Bullis, C. and Stout, K. R. (2000). Organizational socialization: A feminist standpoint approach. In Buzzanell, P. M. (Ed.) *Rethinking organizational & managerial communication from feminist perspectives.* Thousand Oaks, CA: Sage.

Burns, J. M. (1978). *Leadership.* New York: Harper & Row.

Capra, F. (1983). *The tao of physics.* New York: Bantam.

DePree, M. (1992). *Leadership jazz.* New York: Dell.

Deetz, S. A. (1992). *Democracy in an age of corporate colonization.* Albany, NY: SUNY Press.

Deming, W. E. (1986). *Out of the crisis.* Cambridge, MA: Massachusetts Institute of Technology Center for Advanced Engineering Study.

Donaldson, T. (1982). *Corporations and morality.* Englewood Cliffs, NJ: Prentice-Hall.

DuBrin, A. J. (1990). *Essentials of management* (2nd ed.). Cincinnati, OH: South-Western Publishing.

Durant, W. (1933). *The story of philosophy.* New York: Garden City Publishing.

Duska, R. F. (1993). Aristotle: A pre-modern post-modern? Implications for business ethics. *Business Ethics Quarterly, 3,* 227-249.

Emerson, R. W. (1983). *Essays and lectures.* New York: Library of America.

Ferm, V. (Ed.). (1965). *History of philosophical systems.* Totowa, NJ: Littlefield, Adams & Co.

Finnis, J. (1983). *Fundamentals of ethics.* Washington, D.C.: Georgetown University Press.

Fleishman, E. A., Mumford, M. D., Zaccaro, S. J., Levin, K. Y., Korotkin, A. L., & Hein, M. B. (1991). Taxonomic efforts in the description of leadership behavior: A synthesis and functional interpretation. *The Leadership Quarterly, 2,* 245-287.

Foote, S. (1958). *The Civil War: A narrative.* New York: Random House.

Forbes, P. (1991, October). Are you a born leader? *National Petroleum News,* p. 70.

Foster, W. (1986) *The reconstruction of leadership.* Victoria, Australia: Deakin University Press.

Frankl, V. E. (1969). *Man's search for meaning.* (I. Lasch, Trans.). New York: Washington Square Press.

Friedman, M. (1970, September 13). The social responsibility of business is to increase its profits. *New York Magazine, 33*, p. 126.

Gale, R. F. (1969). *Developmental behavior.* New York: Macmillan.

Gastil, J. (1994). A definition and illustration of democratic leadership. *Human Relations, 47*, 953-975.

Gemmill, G., & Oakley, J. (1992). Leadership: An alienating social myth? *Human Relations, 45*, 113-129.

Giddens, A. (1987). *Social theory and modern sociology.* Stanford, CA: Stanford University Press.

Giddens, A. (1982). *Profiles and critiques in social theory.* Berkeley, CA: University of California Press.

Graham, J. (1991). Servant-leadership in organizations: Inspirational and moral. *The Leadership Quarterly, 2*, 105-119.

Green, R. M. (1993). Business ethics as a postmodern phenomenon. *Business Ethics Quarterly, 3*, 219-225.

Greenleaf, R. K. (1995). Servant leadership. In J. T. Wren (Ed.). *The leader's companion: Insights on leadership through the ages*, pp. 18-23. New York: The Free Press.

Handy, C. (1993). *Understanding organizations.* New York: Oxford University Press.

Harré, R. (1970). *The principles of scientific thinking.* Chicago: University of Chicago Press.

Harré, R., Clarke, D., & DeCarlo, N. (1985). *Motives and mechanisms.* London: Methuen.

Harris, M. (1968). *The rise of anthropological theory.* New York: Thomas Y, Crowell Company.

Henderson, J. E. & Brookhart, S. M. (1996). Leader authenticity: Key to organizational climate, health and perceived leader effectiveness. *The Journal of Leadership Studies, 3*(4), 87-101.

Hobbes, T. (1962). *Leviathan.* New York: Collier Books.

Hofstede, G. (1980). *Culture's consequences: International differences in work-related values.* Beverly Hills, CA: Sage.

House, R. J., & Aditya, R. M. (1997). The social scientific study of leadership: Quo vadis? *Leadership Quarterly, 23*, 3, 409-464.

Hunt, J. G. (1991). *Leadership: A new synthesis.* Newbury Park: Sage.

Hutchins, R. (1936). *The higher learning in America.* New Haven, CT: Yale University Press.

Jackall, R. (1988). *Moral mazes: The world of corporate managers.* New York: Oxford University Press.

Jantsch, E. (1980). *The self-organizing universe: Scientific and human implications of the emerging paradigm of evolution.* Elmsford, NY: Pergamon.

Jung, D. I., Bass, B. M., & Sosik, J. J. (1995). Bridging leadership and culture: A theoretical consideration of transformational leadership and collectivistic cultures. *The Journal of Leadership Studies, 2*(4), 3-18.

Katzenbach, J. R., & Smith, D. K. (1992). The delicate balance of team leadership. *The McKinsey Quarterly, 4,* 128-142.

Kaufman, H. (1973). *Administrative feedback in monitoring subordinates' behavior.* Washington, D.C.: Brookings Institution.

Kellert, S. H. (1993). *In the wake of chaos.* Chicago: University of Chicago Press.

Kiel, L. D. (1994). *Managing chaos and complexity in government.* San Francisco: Jossey-Bass.

Kirkpatrick, S. A. & Locke, E. A. (1991). Leadership: Do traits matter? *Academy of Management Executive, 5,* 48-60.

Klenke, K. (1993). Leadership education at the great divide: Crossing into the twenty-first century. *The Journal of Leadership Studies, 1*(1), 112-127.

Kostner, J. (1994). *Virtual leadership.* New York: Warner Books.

Kotter, J. P. (1988). *The leadership factor.* New York: The Free Press.

Kroeber, A. & Kluckhohn, C. (1952). Culture: A critical review of concepts and definitions. *Papers of the Peabody Museum of American Archaeology and Ethnology,* Vol. 47. Cambridge, Mass.: Harvard University.

Kuhn, T. S. (1970). *The structure of scientific revolutions,* (2nd ed). Chicago: University of Chicago Press.

Kunda, G. (1992). *Engineering culture.* Philadelphia: Temple University Press.

Legge, J. (1962). *The texts of Taoism (*from *The sacred books of the East,* Vol. XXXIX, originally published by Oxford University Press in 1891). New York: Dover.

Lewin, K. (1950). The consequences of an authoritarian and democratic leadership. In A. W. Gouldner (Ed.), *Studies in leadership.* New York: Harper & Row, 409-417.

Locke, J. (1947). *An essay concerning human understanding* (Edited by R. Wilburn). New York: Dutton.

Machiavelli, N. (1981). *The prince* (G. Bull, Trans.). Middlesex, England: Penguin Books.

Machiavelli, N. (1950). *The discourses* (C. E. Detmold, Trans.). New York: Random House.

MacIntyre, A. (1984). *After virtue* (2nd Ed.). Notre Dame, IN: University of Notre Dame Press.

McCleary, R. C. (1994). Against ethics. *Philosophy Today, 38,* 440-446.

McSweeney, B. (2002). Hofstede's model of national cultural differences and their consequences: A triumph of faith--a failure of analysis. *Human Relations, 55,* 89-118.

Mill, J.S. (1910). *Utilitarianism, liberty, and representative government.* London: J.M. Dent & Sons Ltd.

Mintzberg, H. (1982). If you're not serving Bill and Barbara, then you're not serving leadership. In J. G. Hunt, U. Sekaran, & C. A. Schriesheim (Eds.), *Leadership: Beyond establishment views* (pp. 239-250). Carbondale: Southern Illinois University Press.

Mumby, D. K. (2000). Communication, organization, and the public sphere: A feminist perspective. In Buzzanell, P. M. (Ed.) *Rethinking organizational & managerial communication from feminist perspectives.* Thousand Oaks, CA: Sage.

Nicholson, N. (1994). Ethics in organizations: A framework for theory and research. *Journal of Business Ethics, 13,* 581-596.

Nietzsche, F. (1974). *The gay science* (W. Kaufmann, trans.). New York: Vintage Books.

Nozick, R. (1974). *Anarchy, state, and utopia.* New York: Basic Books.

Opler, M. E. (1964). The human being in culture theory. *American Anthropologist, 66*(3), 507-28.

Overman, E. S. (1996). The new sciences of administration: Chaos and quantum theory. *Public Administration Review, 56,* 487-491.

Parry, K. W. (1998). Grounded theory and social process: A new direction for leadership research. *Leadership Quarterly, 9*(1), 85-106.

Pawar, B. S. & Eastman, K. K. (1997). The nature and implications of contextual influences on transformational leadership: A conceptual examination. *Academy of Management Review, 22*(1), 80-109.

Peterson, M. F. & Hunt, J. G. (1997). International perspectives on international leadership. *Leadership Quarterly, 8*(3) 203-232.

Pirsig, R. M. (1991). *Lila: An inquiry into morals.* New York: Bantam.

Pirsig, R. M. (1975). *Zen and the art of motorcycle maintenance.* New York: Bantam.

Plato, (1951). *The symposium.* (W. Hamilton, Trans.) Middlesex, England: Penguin.

Rachels, J. (1986). *The elements of moral philosophy.* New York: Random House.

Rasmussen, D. M. (1993). Business ethics and postmodernism: A response. *Business Ethics Quarterly, 3,* 271-277.

Rawls, J. (1971). *A theory of justice.* Cambridge: Harvard University Press.

Rost, J. C. (1995). Leadership: A discussion about ethics. *Business Ethics Quarterly, 5*(1), 129-142.

Rost, J. C. (1993). Leadership development in the new millennium. *The Journal of Leadership Studies, 1*(1), 92-110.

Rost, J. C. (1991). *Leadership for the twenty-first century.* New York: Praeger.

Runkle, G. (1982) *Ethics: An examination of contemporary moral problems.* New York: Holt, Rinehart and Winston.

Russell, B. (1972). *A history of Western philosophy.* New York: Simon & Schuster.

Schein, E. H. (1992). *Organizational culture and leadership* (2nd Ed.). San Francisco, CA: Jossey-Bass.

Schein, E. H. (1986). *Organizational culture and leadership.* San Francisco, CA: Jossey-Bass.

Shaw, W. H. & Barry, V. (2001). *Moral issues in business* (8th ed.). Belmont, CA: Wadsworth.

Shelton, K. (Ed.) (1997). *A new paradigm of leadership.* Provo, UT: Executive Excellence Publishing.

Sparrowe, R. T. & Liden, R. C. (1997). Process and structure in leader-member exchange. *Academy of Management Review, 22*(2), 522-552.

Stogdill, R. M. (1948). Personal factors associated with leadership: A survey of the literature. *Journal of Psychology, 25,* 35-71.

Takala, T. (1998). Plato on leadership. *Journal of Business Ethics, 17*(7), 785-798.

Taylor, F. W. (1911). *Principles of scientific management.* New York: Harper & Brothers.

Tichy, N. M. (1983). *Managing strategic change: Technical, political, and cultural dynamics.* New York: Wiley & Sons.

Tolstoy, L. (1952). War and peace (L. Maude & A. Maude, Trans.). In R. M. Hutchins (Ed.). *Great books of the Western World.* Chicago: Encyclopedia Britannica, Inc.

Tucker, R. (1981). *Politics as leadership.* Columbia, MO: University of Missouri Press.

Wallace, W. M. (1995). *Soul of the Lion.* Gettysburg, PA: Stan Clark Military Books.

Weber, M. (1947). *The theory of social and economic organization.* (Trans. by A. M. Henderson & T. Parsons). New York: The Free Press.

Wheatley, M. J. (1994). *Leadership and the new science.* San Francisco: Berrett-Koehler Publishers.

White, L. A. (1948). Man's control over civilization: An anthropocentric illusion. *The Scientific Monthly, 66,* 235-247.

Wills, G. (1994). *Certain trumpets.* New York: Simon & Schuster.

Winter, D. (1991). A motivational model of leadership: Predicting long-term management success from TAT measures of power, motivation, and responsibility. *The Leadership Quarterly, 2,* 67-80.

Wittgenstein, L. (1958). *Philosophical investigations,* 2nd ed. (G. E. M. Anscombe, Trans.). New York: Macmillan.

Wren, J. T. (1995). The problem of cultural leadership: The lessons of the Dead Leaders Society and a new definition of leadership. *The Journal of Leadership Studies, 2*(4), 122-139.

Wren, J. T. (1994). Teaching leadership: The art of the possible. *The Journal of Leadership Studies, 1*(2), 73-93.

Yammarino, F, J. (1995). Dyadic leadership. *The Journal of Leadership Studies, 2,*(4), 50-74.

Yukl, G. & Van Fleet, D. D. (1992). Theory and research on leadership in organizations. In M. D. Dunnette & L. M. Hough (Eds.). *Handbook of industrial and organizational psychology* (2nd. ed.) Vol. 3, Palo Alto, CA: Consulting Psychologists Press, Inc., 147-197.

Index

About The Author

Richard A. Barker is Associate Professor of Management in Upper Iowa University. His formal education included A.B. in Psychology with a minor in Sociology from San Diego State University in 1974, M.S. in Industrial/Organizational Psychology from San Diego State University in 1976, Ed.D. in Leadership Studies from the University of San Diego in 1990.

During his professional career, Dr. Barker worked under a variety of job titles in the following organizations: General Dynamics/Electronics Division, General Dynamics/Convair, Computer Sciences Corporation, Spectral Dynamics Corporation, California School of Professional Psychology/San Diego Campus, City of San Diego, Navy Personnel Research and Development Center, and Thearle Music Company.

Dr. Barker's teaching career began in the Spring semester of 1977, when he was hired as adjunct faculty by San Diego City College to teach a music history course he had proposed. He was also contracted to teach 20th Century Music Literature and Beginning Voice, and taught in SDCC continuously for over nine years. In January of 1979, Dr. Barker was hired as adjunct faculty to teach in Alfred North Whitehead College of the University of Redlands. He taught a large variety of graduate and undergraduate courses in several programs steadily for a period of twelve years. Because of the retrenchment occurring in the aerospace industry in 1991, he sought a full time teaching position, and accepted a position with Marist College in Poughkeepsie, NY. In 1998, Dr. Barker moved to Iowa, and accepted his current position with Upper Iowa University in the Fall of 2000. In addition to articles published in various academic journals, he has written two novels.

Dr. Barker played electric bass and guitar professionally during the decades of the '60s and '70s, and has been a lifelong member of the American Federation of Musicians. He currently plays the tuba as an amateur in community bands, in brass quintets, and in the UIU wind ensemble. He wrote "I Just Got Here From Kansas And They're Laughing At Me Polka." It was not a big hit.